MARCO POLO

SINGAPORE

www.marco-polo.com

新加坡艺术之家
Tiger
宏
CHINATOWN SEAFOOD RESTAURANT
6222
Tiger Beer
$5.50 /bt
Carlsberg Beer
$6.20 /bt
Beck's Beer
鱼虾

2224
COMBO B
COMBO A
TO A TIGER IN EVERY GET-TOGETHER

SYMBOLS

INSIDER TIP	Insider Tip
★	Highlight
●●●●	Best of...
	Scenic view
	Responsible travel: fair trade and ecology
(*)	Telephone numbers that are not toll-free

PRICE CATEGORIES HOTELS

Expensive	over 175 S$
Moderate	95–175 S$
Budget	under 95 S$

The prices are for two in a double room per night without breakfast

PRICE CATEGORIES RESTAURANTS

Expensive	over 48 S$
Moderate	24–48 S$
Budget	under 24 S$

The prices are for a starter, main course and non-alcoholic drink

 On the cover: The amazing Marina Bay p. 39, 76 | In Peranakan pots p. 69

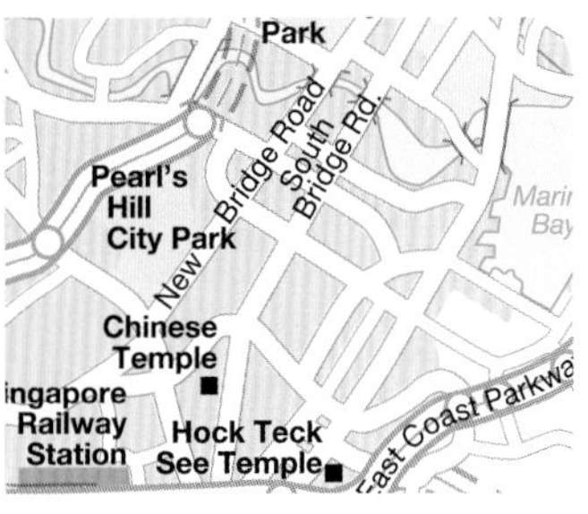

DID YOU KNOW?

Open-air art → p. 36
New land → p. 43
Relax & Enjoy → p. 46
Keep fit! → p. 55
Focus on sport → p. 61
Gourmet restaurants → p. 66
Local specialities → p. 70
Books & Films → p. 86
Luxury hotels → p. 94
Public holidays → p. 117
Addresses in Singapore → p. 122

MAPS IN THE GUIDEBOOK

(128 A1) Page numbers and coordinates refer to the street atlas
(0) Site/address located off the map. Coordinates are also given for places that are not marked on the street atlas.

(🕮 A–B 2–3) Refers to the removable pull-out map
(🕮 a–b 2–3) Refers to the additional map on the removable pull-out map

INSIDE FRONT COVER:
The best Highlights

INSIDE BACK COVER:
Public transportation route map

The best MARCO POLO Insider Tips

Our top 15 Insider Tips

INSIDER TIP Acquired tastes
Savour and savvy: at the *Local Food Trail* in the Hawker Centre of the ION Orchard acquire some Asian tastes under expert guidance → **p. 66**

INSIDER TIP Magic spirals
The wooden *Henderson Waves,* Singapore's highest pedestrian bridge, winds at treetop height through a jungle park → **p. 56**

INSIDER TIP Rock 'n' roll on the waterfront
Singaporean bands give free concerts when night falls at the weekend on the open-air stage in front of the *Esplanade Culture Centre* → **p. 106**

INSIDER TIP Occupied Singapore
Memories of times past at the *Old Ford Factory:* here where cars once left the production line, you will gain deep insight into life in the city state during the time of the Japanese occupation → **p. 60**

INSIDER TIP Be amused with the drag queen
Kumar, Singapore's top drag queen, makes fun of everything her countrymen hold sacred. (S)he is definitely the only one who can get away with it → **p. 89**

INSIDER TIP Tasty Laksa
Singapore's traditional dish is much more than just noodle soup – and it tastes best at the *328 Katong Laksa* snack bar (photo right) → **p. 69**

INSIDER TIP In the Peranakan world
Immerse yourself in the life of Singapore's early immigrants; you will find all of the information you need on the Peranakan culture in the *Katong Antique House* → **p. 102**

INSIDER TIP Spinning round in circles
A top-class Chinese restaurant, the *Prima Tower,* revolves above an old flour mill. The establishment's famous Peking duck tastes all the better in the 1960s ambience and with the spectacular view → **p. 67**

INSIDER TIP Bargaining a must!

Paradise for shopaholics: the traders at the *Queensway Shopping Centre* offer sports shoes and eyewear at special prices in their typically jam-packed Asian shops. Goods are original products by popular sports brands, 20 percent below city-centre prices → **p. 77**

INSIDER TIP Halls full of furniture

Buyers have been plundering Asia's antiques shops for years; much is now sold out. But at *Tan Boon Liat Building* you still have the chance to find just what you're after among the old and reproduction furniture, accessories and carpets → **p. 79**

INSIDER TIP See and be seen

Guaranteed to cause a stir! Send the folks back home your favourite photo of Singapore – as a *postage stamp*. But let the recipient in on the secret: make sure the little gem on your holiday greetings don't end up unnoticed in the waste paper basket → **p. 123**

INSIDER TIP Made to measure

The oldest shirt-maker in Singapore, Cyc, not only produces the best men's shirts – and ladies' blouses – in the city but also repairs frayed cuffs and collars; years later, if desired → **p. 80**

INSIDER TIP Bales of material

If you love fabrics, the thrill of the hunt, and haggling to your hearts content, make sure to visit the Chinese stores in *People's Park* (photo left) → **p. 80**

INSIDER TIP Cheers!

Cucumber juice, pepper, chocolate? At *Bar Stories* in the hip district Kampong Glam no ingredient is too exotic for the barkeeper for your personal dream cocktail → **p. 85**

INSIDER TIP Country outing at the port

The most beautiful *food court* in town is located by the sea on the roof of the Vivo City shopping centre and looks like an old Chinese village → **p. 65**

BEST OF...

GREAT PLACES FOR FREE

Discover new places and save money

FOR FREE

Free Friday

On Friday between 6 and 9pm you do not have to buy a ticket to go to the revered *Singapore Art Museum*. You can start the weekend by admiring the art of South-East Asia and the special exhibitions free of charge → p. 37

Refreshing water

Each restaurant in sweltering Singapore can turn out to be a real oasis; since you can generally get free iced water to drink. Just ask for it if it is not offered automatically. Your glass will be refilled as often as you like during the meal → p. 71

Waterside panorama

At weekends, Chinese residents fly their kites on the roof of the Marina Barrage. With good reason: from here, you get a fabulous view of the skyscrapers, the new Botanic Gardens and the sea → p. 42

Playtime

Many attractions for children have to be paid for in expensive Singapore. But the younger generation can romp around for free in the old Botanic Gardens: *Jacob Ballas Children's Garden* provides climbing frames, a water playground and a delightful café next door → p. 114

Free titbits

You can sample the local specialities such as biscuits, grilled pork and mooncakes (photo) at the stands set up in the special area in the basement of the *Takashimaya* department store on the days before important Chinese festivals → p. 76

Work up a sweat for free

Are you fit and not put off by a little heat? Then you should give some of Singapore's sports a try – from dragon-boat racing to a so-called 'Prosperity Run', which should make you wealthy! The *Singapore Sports Hub* offers free two-hour sessions, mostly on Saturday mornings, when you can have a go at these and more besides → p. 18

Dots in guidebook refer to 'Best of...' tips

ONLY IN SINGAPORE
Unique experiences

Eat like the locals
Forget all about the gourmet restaurants and eat seated on a plastic stool in one of the countless food courts or 'hawker centres'. Do not worry about the quality: taxes and rent are very low so that makes it possible for the stall owners to serve high-class traditional food for a couple of dollars. One of the best hawker centres in the city is *Makansutra Gluttons Bay* directly next to the Esplanade → p. 66

Gamble like the Chinese
The Chinese love to gamble. Spend an evening with the locals and join in the fun. The best place is in the Marina Bay Sands complex where the charm of Las Vegas goes hand in hand with the compulsive gambling of the Chinese → p. 23, 42

Black delights
It is true; they do look like they were dipped into axle grease. Put on an old, dark shirt (to hide the spots) mingle with the Singaporeans and sink your teeth into the *black pepper crabs* at the East Coast Seafood Centre → p. 68

Speed along the coast
If you want to find out what Singapore is really like, pedal along the surfaced promenade of the *East Coast*. Just take a taxi as far as Marine Cove where you can rent bikes and inline skates every few hundred yards; all the rental facilities are equally good → p. 55

Shop until you drop
The Singaporeans love shopping – the real spending variety or just window shopping. Do not only stroll through the main malls, visit the small merchants on Pagoda Street in Chinatown or in the side streets of Serangoon Road in Little India → p. 46, 51

Floral glory
Singapore's national flower is the orchid (photo). Prominent visitors to the city state are often honoured with a new variety named after them. One recent addition you will be able to admire in the beautiful *Orchid Garden in the old Botanic Gardens* is the *Dendrobium Angela Merkel*. The German Chancellor was one of the first to inhale the perfume of its violet and mint-coloured blossoms in 2011 → p. 57

BEST OF...

AND IF IT RAINS?

Activities to brighten your day

● *Feel at home*

There are fully grown trees from good old Europe in the cool glasshouses in the *Gardens by the Bay*. The flora is fascinatingly displayed, and it is well worth spending an entire rainy day here sheltered by the glass → p. 41

● *In the jungle*

Of course, you will get wet here, so put on your flip-flops, shorts and a light top. You will also need an umbrella to protect you from the monsoon rain. Wandering through the old rainforest in the *Botanic Gardens* becomes a very special tropical experience → p. 57

● *Dry shopping*

No matter how heavy the monsoon rain is, you will be able to walk for miles through the shopping centres without your feet getting wet. Most of the malls on Orchard Road are connected with each other underground. Start at *Wheelock Place* and make your way to the *Ion* with its gallery of luxury shops (photo) → p. 72, 75

● *Art in full bloom*

The *Art Science Museum* is the newest and most impressive institution of its kind in Singapore: the organisers acquire the world's most fascinating exhibitions to be shown in the gigantic white lotus blossom in front of Marina Bay Sands → p. 39

● *Sweet comforter*

Bad weather – bad mood? Take a taxi to the *PS. Café*. There are only bigger slices of cake in Australia! You sit under tropical trees and listen to the falling raindrops → p. 64

● *Snow instead of rain*

If you are a person who prefers snow to rain, head for *Snow City* in the *Science Centre* complex where you will find a ski slope and can rent all the necessary gear → p. 115

RELAX AND CHILL OUT

Take it easy and spoil yourself

● ***Born again***

Too long on the plane? Have you 'shopped till you dropped'? Let yourself be pampered at the *Beauty Emporium at House*. They also sell some interesting care products, too → **p. 46**

● ***Sightseeing light***

No matter whether you choose to set sail in an old wooden boat from *River Cruise* or a bumpy, amphibian vehicle from *Duck & Hippo*, it is always a wonderful experience to be taken on a cruise of Singapore's waterways and marvel at the breathtaking views of the city from the water (photo) → **p. 115, 125**

● ***Silent observer***

The fragrance of joss sticks and the rapt devotion of the faithful in the *Thian Hock Keng Temple* in the middle of the hustle and bustle of the metropolis will help you get your feet back on the ground. Here, nobody minds onlookers → **p. 49**

● ***Romantic sundowner***

The sun sinks into the sea behind the tropical trees, the birds' twittering heralds the coming evening and the waiters in the outdoor lounge of *The Knolls* at the luxurious *Capella Hotel* on Sentosa know exactly what their guests want without having to ask → **p. 67**

● ***Hollywood reclining***

The only place where it is more pleasant to watch a film than in the *Golden Village* in the *Vivo City* shopping centre is at home on your sofa: you can make yourself comfy in the reclining chairs and even order dinner. → **p. 57**

● ***Cycle deluxe***

Of course, it is easy to get around in Singapore by underground, bus or taxi, but it is much more fun and very comfortable to be driven around town in a rickshaw. All of your senses can focus on the life going on around you; you will not have to walk far and avoid all the pushing and shoving. Furthermore, find out, which tales the drivers can tell you about old Singapore → **p. 125**

INTRODUCTION

DISCOVER SINGAPORE!

Asia for beginners? A ***city of sterile buildings*** with no character, without any soul? Few other places in South-East Asia are laden down with as many clichés as the five-million metropolis of Singapore. Everybody thinks they know the small ***tropical island*** – 42 km (26 mi) long and a maximum of 23 km (14 mi) wide – at the south-eastern tip of the Asian continent: most visitors immediately think of marathon shopping sprees on Orchard Road. Or maybe about the famous ***Singapore Sling*** cocktail, a relic from times long past when the city was a British crown colony. And there is hardly a visitor who does not joke about the ***'fine city'***, the wonderful town with all its penalties for wrongdoing.

Of course, there is a certain element of truth to these clichés. The city actually is ***'Asia light'*** because it does all it can to make Europeans feel at home in no time. Singapore has ***metamorphosised*** again over the past few years. The scruffy harbour town that transformed itself with iron discipline into a colonial metropolis and then rose to become the centre of South-East Asia has blossomed into a ***global, cosmopolitan city***. It is easy to explore Singapore on your own, you will be able to eat and drink wherever the urge hits you it and feel ***safe*** everywhere in the city. What is more, you will always

Photo: Gardens by the Bay

meet ***friendly passers-by*** who will be happy to help and to proudly tell you about how life really is in their homeland.

It's no wonder that some 15 million visitors come to this tropical paradise every year, a great many of them from English-speaking countries. They enjoy the courteous service in the hotels, relish the colonial flair and make the most of the hypermodern luxury the city has to offer: you can hear the cash registers in the stores ringing from ten in the morning until ten at night, seven days a week. Those who just devote themselves to shopping sprees, however, will go home with a superficial impression that does not do justice to Singapore. The ***multicultural city*** – 74 percent of the population is Chinese, 13 percent Malay, and nine percent Indian – is a genuine Asian metropolis. Buddhists, Muslims and Hindus live alongside each other ***in harmony***. ***Two public holidays*** were selected from ***each religion***, and they apply everywhere on the island. That is one reason for Hindus celebrating Christmas, Christians Chinese New Year, and Muslims the Hindu Deepavali festival – the other is, because it boosts sales figures. While exploring districts such as ***Chinatown*** or ***Little India***, visitors will be able to get a glimpse of life behind the modern, Western facades of the metropolis that, at first glance, seems to characterise Singapore. Everyday life is still determined by the traditions of the Singaporeans' home countries. Women go shopping in Little India in dazzlingly ***colourful saris***, in Chinatown you will mainly see elderly ladies going about their business in comfortable Chinese clothing, a pyjama-

Everyday life is determined by traditions from China, India and Malaysia

Singapore shows it is also a truly Asian metropolis in districts such as Chinatown

like blouse and trousers combination. The Malay children look really adorable on their way to the mosque dressed up in their finest clothes.

It can be quite an effort to walk around in the oppressively hot tropical climate, but you will be rewarded with fascinating insights into a completely different world: give the atmosphere in a ***Hindu temple*** time to make its full impact on you, don't just take a quick look inside. The faithful will be happy to tell you about their ***particular deities***; if you are there on Friday, you might even be invited to share a meal. On your stroll through Chinatown, you will not only inhale the fragrance of ***joss sticks*** in the Chinese temples but also on many corners in the district: the perfume essence is stuck into colourful fruit on little altars.

All Singaporeans share a love of fine food

Singapore is developing ***at a faster pace*** than almost any other city on earth. New ***skyscrapers*** and shopping centres spring up ***every month***. Pensioners in fine-rib singlets and businesswomen in their elegant suits meet at the same ***hawker stall*** on the corner at lunchtime: everybody is united in their love of good food – young and old, rich and poor, Chinese, Malays and Indians.

Singapore is an international financial and commercial centre and is completely justified in seeing itself as the ***hub of the entire region***, the city everything revolves around, not only to the benefit of its immediate neighbours Indonesia and Malaysia, but all of South-East Asia. More than two-thirds of all the goods shipped from Europe to South-East Asia pass through Singapore's ***impressive container terminal*** on their way to their final destination in other countries in the area. Singapore is also a haven of stability in a volatile region. The governing People's Action Party (PAP), assisted by media aligned to the state, remains benevolent as long as nobody questions their opinion. The party of the autocratic, but charismatic, founder of the state Lee Kuan Yew, which ***practically monopolises*** the main positions, careers and influence, makes life for opposition parties difficult. However, a surprising ***opening process*** started in 2011: the PAP lost considerable influence in the elections and the opposition candidates taught them to be wary. The well-educated and widely travelled Singaporeans criticised the autocracy in their country and those who were suffering protested

about the permanent increase in prices in the luxurious metropolis. At the same time, the government realised that the protest movement of the Arab Spring might well be imitated in the neighbouring countries such as Malaysia. Today, every move of the Singapore government is widely covered in the ***blogs of critics*** and political opponents. The PAP took the plunge and started moving forwards. The salaries of the ministers and president were cut by around one third, but remain high. Price increases are being combated by the increasing value of the Singapore dollar – which has made the country an expensive destination for European travellers. The influx of foreign workers was massively curbed – Singaporeans are given top priority. They are also to receive ***even better education*** to guarantee that they have jobs in the future. Singapore's famously effective Economic Development Board aims at having the city state become a 'control tower' for Asia. This is where the managers of the international concerns – which produce in the neighbouring countries to take advantage of the lower wages there – should have their offices, this should be the location of research and development centres, and where ***top universities*** mould students to become the region's managers.

The city state's aim is to develop into the 'control tower' of Asia

In spite of the noticeable opening, there is not the same freedom that one sees in Europe: the trade unions have been transformed into instruments of the government, **the media are censored**, there is no freedom of assembly. However, the majority of the population is ***satisfied*** with their government, even though there is an increasing gap between the rich and poor. In spite of the economic slump, the unemployment rate is under control, there is a well-educated middle class, a ***safety net*** of social benefits and egalitarian, ***social housing schemes***. In addition, all of the neighbouring countries are envious of the island state's ***excellent health system***. There is a low crime rate and the subjective feeling of safety is much higher than in other metropolises. This makes staying in Singapore extremely pleasant – not only for visitors who are on their first trip to Asia.

Singa Pura, ***Lion City***, was the name chosen by the discoverer of this coastal village, the Indian Prince Nila Utama, in the 13th century after he had seen an awe-inspiring creature that he thought was a lion in the dense tropical forest. 'Singa' is the Sanskrit word for lion. On account of its favourable geographic position on the Malacca Straits, Siamese, Indian, Javan and Malay merchants turned this spot into a small trading centre.

When he landed there in January 1819, the British colonial administrator ***Sir Thomas Stamford Raffles*** immediately recognised the strategic importance of the village with its around 300 inhabitants, which at the time belonged to the Sultanate of Johor on the southern tip of Malaya. Raffles acquired the island for the ***East India Company*** and laid the foundation for Singapore's future. In the following 50 years, Indian prisoners cleared the malaria-infested jungle, built streets and canals. Chinese coolies carried ivory and spices, tea, silk, precious wood and opium, and later tin and rubber, from the ships to the warehouses. By 1911, Singapore's population had increased to

Half lion, half fish and completely white, the Merlion majestically spurts water into Marina Bay

around 250,000 and included 48 ethnic groups. Most came from South China; many others from Indonesia, Malaysia and India.

For the British colonial powers, Singapore was an extremely important and supposedly perfectly ***fortified base – impregnable*** from the sea. However, as part of their ***campaign to subjugate*** Asia, the Japanese cleverly resorted to – bicycles! They pedalled down the Malay Peninsula and conquered Singapore, which was unprotected from that side, on 15 February 1942. ***Japanese forces*** ruled the island with extreme brutality for three and a half years until their capitulation on 21 August 1945. That is when the British returned, and Singapore became a ***crown colony***. The mythical beast that Prince Nila Utama thought he saw was chosen to be the city's symbol: it is called the Merlion and has the head of a lion and body of a fish.

The conquerors came by bicycle

Statues of the ***Merlion*** welcome visitors to Sentosa, ***Marina Bay*** and the souvenir shops. The journey from the airport to the city is full of promises – and Singapore keeps them all: palms sway in the breeze, you catch a glimpse of the glittering sea on the left, and all bridges are covered with bougainvilleas. Visitors are surprised and enchanted by the ***beautiful floral decorations*** in this well cared-for city where it is so pleasant to live. There is always something new on the agenda: the first ever night-time event in Formula 1 racing is held here, two casinos and the Universal Amusement Park also attract visitors and the world's largest museum of south-east Asian art opened here in 2015.

WHAT'S HOT

1 A hand for crafts

Design city Singapore has become fertile soil for sharp Asian design. Much is driven by the *Lasalle College of the Arts (McNally Street | www.lasalle.edu.sg)*. What's more interesting, however, is the new showcase for young Singaporean designers – with municipal backing and located right on Orchard Road – *Keepers (daily 11am–10pm | Orchard Road/Cairnhill | www.keepers.com.sg | MRT NS 23 Somerset)* has a huge range of lovingly crafted, often quirky items, from perfume, through tableware, jewellery to fashion – stuff you can't find anywhere else.

Bubbles and Heels 2

Raise your glasses, ladies Wednesday is the day of the by no means 'weaker sex'. In Singapore, Wednesday is *Ladies Night*. Most bars and discos offer them free drinks and free admission; only the men have to pay. The watchword here is 'Bubbles and Heels' – in other words, champagne and elegant footwear. Find out about times and locations at *www.citynomads.com* or *www.timeout.com/singapore*.

Sporting tasters 3

Oddball sports Have you ever played *Speedminton*? Or taken part in a *'Prosperity Run'*, which aims to lead you on the road to riches? Would you like to paddle a dragon boat? You can try this and more at the new ● *Sports Hub Singapore (2 Stadium Walk)*. The stadium complex offers amateur athletes a host of taster courses, usually on Saturday mornings. Asian sports take centre-stage – have a go at one for a couple of hours, guided by great trainers and for free. Book your sporting adventure in advance under *www.sportshub.com.sg/community/Pages/experience-sports.aspx*.

There are lots of new things to discover in Singapore. A few of the most interesting are listed below

Cooking with convicts

4

Rehabilitation On his home turf, Jamie Oliver took British kids off the streets and trained them as chefs. In Singapore, the city state with the draconian penal system, Benny Se Teo has made it his mission to re-integrate former convicts into society – as chefs. The ex-cons now run eight restaurants known as the *Eighteen Chefs (e.g. at 2 Handy Road | #B1–19/20 | The Cathay | www.eighteenchefs.com)*. But they would like to spread their concept throughout Asia and, one day perhaps, around the globe. The food is tasty, freshly cooked and reasonably priced. And if you take the time, you can hear some moving stories from the lives of those who would otherwise disappear behind Singapore's glittering façades.

Hanging gardens

5

Urban greenery The city is a veritable sea of buildings. Singapore does not want to be perceived like this, however, and therefore the metropolis is allowing itself to become overgrown – on purpose. Hanging gardens are being planted to cover a growing number of façades. Research institutes are testing the vertical cultivation of vegetables, to enable the city and its residents to rapidly become less dependent on imports. Canals are being renaturated, such as in *Bishan-Ang Mo Kio Park,* created by landscape architects to the north of the city – much to the delight of local residents. Parks like this are currently being created in Singapore every six months or so. Right in the centre, there are also beautiful examples of these new green façades, such as the *Parkroyal on Pickering*. Look for other green sites at *www.nparks.gov.sg.*

IN A NUTSHELL

ABBREVIATIONS

Travel into the city with the MRT from the HDB instead of being caught in a traffic jam on the blocked PIE and then having to pay at the ERP? If that sounds Greek to you, you need a crash course in Singapore speak because it is simply teeming with these kinds of abbreviations. You can learn them as you go along but new ones are always being added to the list. The solution: MRT is the Mass Rapid Transit Authority, the underground and suburban trains. HDB stands for the Housing Development Board, which sells state flats. It is also used as a synonym for the high-rise towers in the satellite towns. PIE is the Pan Island Expressway, one of Singapore's motorways. And ERP means Electronic Road Pricing – a toll system in which fees for road use and many multi-storey car parks are read from a chip card in the car. It is impossible not to notice the bridges with the scanners such as those over Orchard Road.

ART

Art is also part of the new Singapore. The *Biennale* has developed into a permanent prominent event in the arts calendar. Many foreign artists take part and often bring a breath of fresh air into even out-of-the-way areas of the city with their

 Photo: In the Marina Bay Sands shopping centre

From feng shui, kiasu and a passion for malls to the five Cs, the Singlish language and life in a fully air-conditioned wonderland

sculptures and installations. The *Art Stage* art fair opens its doors every year in January: in a mere three days, this offshoot of Art Basel shows everything Asia has to offer in the way of art. A special gallery district was established at the end of 2012, its aim being to further fire enthusiasm in this cultural area and add another interesting facet to the city's image. Twenty – mostly Asian – art dealers have taken up residence in the old colonial buildings of the former *Gillman Barracks,* along with studios, a research centre, several cafés and spaces for special events. However, Singapore's established artists criticise the artificial character of this kind of development. However, despite their scepticism, the gallery will still be interesting for visitors to the city.

CAMPAIGNS

Nothing works without a government campaign. The cleanliness activities of the 1970s are legendary; at the time, a person took up a position next to every public toilet and asked the users if they had flushed properly. At the moment, the government is encouraging Singaporeans to act entrepreneurially. After almost 50 years during which the state regulated everything, personal initiative and creativity are now in demand.

As green as it gets: Singapore's lovely old Botanic Gardens now have a younger counterpart

COFFEE

Learn your coffee ABC's in Singapore: coffee here is known as kopi and is served with milk. Kopi-O is black, with sugar. Kopi-C combines sugar and milk; kopi-peng comes with milk, sugar and ice.

FENG SHUI

The right feng shui is extremely important in Singapore. Feng shui (translated, it means 'wind and water') is the Chinese art of geomantics, recognising those positive and negative influences of a house that influence health and commercial success. Harmony is the magic word and the direction a building faces, the position of its windows and doors is precisely determined. Feng shui walks are offered by several agencies *(www.trailsofindochina.com/singapore/tailored_experiences, www.diethelmtravel.com/packages/singapore-and-fengshui-tour)*.

FIVE CS

Although he is clearly proud of Singapore's achievements, the state's founding father, Lee Kuan Yew, is also sometimes concerned about his people. He was the man who encouraged the Singaporeans to do business and make money – to turn Singapore into what it is today. The other side of the coin is that human relations suffer when attention is focused on one's bank account and personal success defined by the five Cs that are the driving force behind everyone in Singapore: *Career*, *Credit Card*, *Condo* (complete with swimming pool), *Club* (with membership fees of several thousand dollars; the more exclusive the better) and *Car* (import duty make cars far more expensive than they are in Europe).

FOOD

Life is not complete without good food and this applies more to Singapore than anywhere else in the world. The metropolis offers an almost unbelievable choice of different places to go and eat and types of cuisine. There is something to satisfy all tastes and all budgets, from the hawkers – the cookshops, in the food markets that are usually located in the basement or on the top floor of the shopping centres – to the five-star chefs in the Marina Bay Sands Casino Complex. And the quality? Professor Tommy Koh, formerly a Singaporean ambassador, who has made the development of his city his life's work, boasts: 'I consider that our Char Kway Teow (a popular dish of rice noodles, sausages coated with wax and fish paste) and our Laksa (noodle soup) are better than any other noodle dishes in the world. I do not know of any Western salad that can compete with our Rojak (fruit and vegetable salad). And I am sure that, when they are warm and fluffy and eaten with Chicken Curry, our Roti Prata (Indian pancakes) easily beat any pizza I have ever tasted.' He could be right!

GAMBLING

● The Chinese are not the only people who like to gamble but they are especially fond of it. Gambling for money used to be forbidden in Singapore but now the city state has had a complete change of heart. There are two new casinos: the Marina Bay Sands and one at the Resort World Sentosa. Foreigners get in free, but in an attempt to curb their compulsive gambling, Singaporeans have to pay 100 S$. Revenue from gambling in both casino complexes, rather shamefully referred to as 'integrated resorts', lay at around 5.5 bn S$ in 2014 – almost as high as in Las Vegas. However, dyed-in-the-wool Singaporeans are not at all pleased about the new gambling dens. They are afraid that this will lead to women working in the oldest profession and tough guys moving into town.

The love of gambling and search for profit goes so far that the Singapore Straits Times reported that employers sometimes give their workers thousands of dollars and send them to the casinos during working hours to play – and hopefully win – for them. The workers are all in favour: they can spend the day in air-conditioned comfort instead of in the tropical heat and get a cut of ten percent of any winnings. The downside: they can lose their month's wages if the losses are too great.

GARDEN CITY

One is not enough: the city state has had a world-famous Botanic Gardens for many years, which has recently achieved World-Heritage status. But now Singapore has a second, huge botanical garden, built on land reclaimed from the sea. Since the government of the financial centre on the equator is not only rich but also very clever, it is spending around 1 bn S$ on the project. Together with improvements made to the old Botanic Gardens, the small country has invested a good 1.5 bn S$ in green areas – despite the global economic crisis. There is no need for hothouses in this climate, but special greenhouses had to be developed for the Gardens by the Bay where plants from northern countries can flourish at low temperatures. The city state's aim is to develop from being a 'garden city' to a 'city in a garden'. In the past quarter century, the green areas in Singapore have increased from around one third to half of the city's surface area. The Gardens by the Bay spread over an area of 250 acres – half the size of Monaco.

Fresh air is not necessarily the main reason for the massive greening of Singapore: economics play a major role, and the value of green areas and water was painstakingly calculated. The result is that real-estate prices show considerable increases in districts around the green areas – the best argument for increasing the city's garden areas even more. Without doubt, Singapore has now become the greenest city in Asia and probably one of the greenest in the world. Seen from one of the skyscrapers, the roads wind through the city like green thread. The city covers skyscrapers vertically with plants and also uses dozens of reserves and parks for water collection. This is a very agreeable aspect of Singapore. It is also a factor that improves the quality of life in the city and makes it even more attractive for wealthy new citizens. Anybody who has spent time in Manila or Mumbai will really appreciate the greenery here. Especially since it is on the increase. According to the government, by the end of 2030 some 80 percent of all buildings in the city will be 'green' – whatever that means. On the other hand, a huge amounts of energy is needed to cool houses down to as low as 19°C (66°F). Most old private homes and tower blocks have windows that do not close properly and thin walls. This leads to enormous energy wastage and increases Singapore's overall energy costs.

MALL MANIA

The Singaporeans love their shopping malls. The city state has hardly any hinterland and therefore the possibilities for leisure-time activities are limited. Of course, there are sports arenas, nature parks and countless possibilities to use one's free time sensibly – but all appeals have so far been in vain: most Singaporeans spend their spare time in shopping centres. They are open every day and usually from 10am to 10pm. It can even be rather difficult to walk along Orchard Road at the weekend. During the week, you see school children doing their homework in the halls and – even more popular – fast-food restaurants. It is pleasantly cool there and many of the HDB flats are not equipped with air conditioning.

OPPOSITION

Opposition is becoming more vociferous and self-assured. During the last parliamentary elections in Singapore, the opposition fared much better than the government party expected. Even the widely respected foreign minister lost his seat and had to resign from office. Since then, the government has changed its tactics and is attempting to make the city state more open. The aim is to make things more transparent, more humane and not just for the benefit of the rich. This explains why the boss of the underground lines was forced to leave her job after there was a problem with the trains – in earlier days, she would have just sat it out but now there is fear that the people will get angry. That also explains why the prime minister, who was formerly the highest paid in the world with a salary of £1.6 million (2.1 million US$), now only gets £1.1 million (1.4 million US$) a year – this makes him only one of the best paid.

SHOPHOUSES

Some of the traditional shophouses still exist in Little India, in Chinatown, on Arab Street and Boat Quay. The government came to its senses shortly before the last of these houses, which once belonged to the early immigrants, were demolished. Today, most of the shophouses provide space for small stores and pubs. However, there are still families who live the way they did in days gone by. The ground floor is used for storage or as a salesroom and the family lives on the top floor.

SINGLISH

Almost all Singaporeans speak two – and many three or four – languages. It is compulsory to learn the lingua franca, English, in school and the youngsters speak their parents' language – Mandarin, Tamil or Malay – at home. A genuine Singaporean usually also speaks a dialect made up of a mixture of English with scraps of Chinese: Sing-lish. The added syllable *lah*, as in okay-lah, is famous. *Kiasu* is important. The word from Hokkien Chinese means 'fear of losing' – a quality the Singaporeans attribute to themselves. This is what leads to pushing and shoving at sales and also impedes their courage to risk something new. That is why official Singapore is trying to get the Singaporeans to do away with *kiasu*.

WEALTH

In 2013, Singapore's population of around 5.4 million included some 105,000 millionaires (calculated in US dollars). According to the Credit Suisse bank this number would rise to over 400,000 in 2017. Many have become wealthy because the real-estate prices have increased steadily over the past decades. It is thus not that surprising that the children of wealthy parents can be found racing their Ferraris and Lamborghinis at night. However, not everybody is rich: the average income of the top ten percent of the population increased by a hefty 58 percent between 2000 and 2010; overall, average growth was around 48 percent, driven by the big earners. However, the income of the bottom tenth has only increased by ten percent in the same time.

Shop downstairs, home upstairs: this is the charming Chinese version of a 'department store'

SIGHTSEEING

> **CITY WHERE TO START?**
> **Raffles Monument (136 B2)** ***(J4)*:** Start at the memorial to Sir Stamford Raffles in the old Colonial Quarter. The North-South and East-West underground lines stop here. You look across at the banking district, the Asian Civilisations Museum lies in front of you and the Fullerton Hotel is on the right. Chinatown awaits you and just a few steps downriver, you reach Marina Bay with Singapore's new symbol, the Marina Bay Sands complex.

No matter whether you decide to walk between the skyscrapers in the Central Business District, past the small shophouses in Chinatown and Little India or explore the city's many parks and gardens, there is one rule you should bear in mind: do not rush, walk slowly.

On no account, should you make your personal sightseeing programme too full. Even a short stroll can be strenuous in the humid, sticky climate of this tropical city state where the temperature seldom sinks below 30°C (86°F). You will be able to deal better with the high humidity if you take regular breaks and drink a lot of mineral water.

 Photo: Hindu Sri Mariamman temple

Traditional rhythms dominate the lifestyle in Chinatown and Little India – while just a few streets away, the metropolis races

The city is perfectly suited to being explored on foot. Sir Stamford Raffles, the founding father of Singapore, established the Chinatown, Little India and Arab Street districts; he thought it would be a good idea to keep the ethnic groups separated from each other. Today, Singapore's multicultural society would be amused at such notions – there are as many Chinese businessmen in Little India as there are Indian tailors in Chinatown. However, you will still get a feeling of the original character of these different districts as you stroll through them.

Take a leisurely walk around Serangoon Road in Little India and let the friendly merchants tell you all about their exotic goods. In the Thian Hock Keng Temple in Chinatown, you will be shown how it is possible to tell the future with fortune

The map shows the location of the most interesting districts. There is a detailed map of each district on which each of the sights described is numbered.

sticks. As you continue your walk along the river and towards the Esplanade shopping district, you will also experience the flair of the metropolis' former colonial splendour.

Modern Singapore reveals itself on Orchard Road, in the Central Business District and in the newly developed Marina Bay area. In 2010, the two casinos with their gigantic hotels and the Universal Studio amusement park opened their doors on the Sentosa leisure island. They cost more than £5 billion (8.2 billion US$). On top of this came the new law courts, the opening of the enormous National Library and Singapore Management University and the reconstruction of the National Museum. The real highlight, however, is the new Botanic Gardens by the Bay and the Marina Bay Sands complex. The many air-conditioned shopping centres are perfect places to relax from your walk through the city and have a meal. The spotlessly clean, cool MRT underground trains not only take you to destinations in the inner city but are ideal for excursions to the satellite towns. There, among the endless rows of skyscrapers in Pasir Ris, Sembawang and Boon Lay you will be able to explore Singapore's heartland as the island dwellers call this area far away from the inner city. Covered footpaths lead into the high-rise complexes that are mostly surrounded by small shops. The floors of the markets for fresh goods in the basements are kept washed down and this has led to them being known as 'wet markets'.

Art is still a relatively new chapter in the history of the city but the government has recognised that it needs to catch up in this area. The world's largest museum for south-east Asian art, die National Gallery Singapore, opened its doors in 2015. The former Supreme Court and City Hall were gutted and merged together for this purpose. The former Gillman Barracks were transformed into a gallery district. Exhibitions and auctions complete the picture. The *Esplanade Theatres on the Bay* stage concerts, plays and changing exhibitions. The delightfully renovated Victoria Theatre and its concert hall are worthy additions to the cultural scene.

The city attempts to create a link between Asian and Western culture that appeals to all ethnic groups. This is not a simple matter. The Singaporeans are all descendants of immigrants from countries of a very different culture and they often find it difficult to fully appreciate each other's cultural assets and achievements. While performances of Indian dance and Peking opera have little appeal for other groups, street-theatre groups – now permitted on Orchard Road – attract a mixed audience. In spite of the goal of developing an intrinsic Singaporean cultural identity, it is important for the multinational state to preserve the artistic heritage of its Chinese, Malay and Indian peoples; you will find information on all activities under *www.yoursingapore.com.*

There are around 140 large churches, mosques and temples in Singapore, plus dozens of smaller places of worship. They are all open to the public. You must take off your shoes before entering a mosque or temple and, especially in Muslim houses of worship, women should be ap-

MARCO POLO HIGHLIGHTS

★ **Asian Civilisations Museum**
The entire region on show for all to see
→ p. 32

★ **National Gallery Singapore**
The world's largest museum for modern south-east Asian art
→ p.34

★ **Orchard Road**
Superlative shopping boulevard → p. 35

★ **Gardens by the Bay**
Singapore's newest green landmark. For many, the most beautiful park in Asia → p. 40

★ **Raffles Hotel**
The institution among the hotels in Singapore
→ p. 36

★ **Marina Bay Sands**
Almost blinding luxury → p. 42

★ **Chinatown**
Renovated shop-houses and Clarke Quay for night owls → p. 46

★ **Sri Mariamman Temple**
A colourful Hindu house of worship, popular for weddings
→ p. 48

★ **Thian Hock Keng Temple**
A glittering gem
→ p. 49

★ **Little India**
Between gods and spices → p. 51

★ **Resort World Sentosa**
A real must for kids: the Universal Studios amusement park → p. 54

★ **Singapore Zoological Gardens, Night Safari & River Safari**
Visit the animals in the large enclosures during the day – and at night
→ p. 60

propriately dressed. The main prayer halls of the mosques are reserved for men. Follow the locals' lead in the temples; you can take part in all activities, buy joss sticks and put them in the vessels in front of the altars and join the faithful as they walk around (always to the left!). Leave a small donation; the churches, temples and mosques depend on them. *The houses of worship are usually open all day*

COLONIAL QUARTER

The heart of the city developed along its earlier lifeline, the Singapore River. The most beautiful restored colonial buildings can be seen on its banks and it is only natural that this is where you will find the statue of the city's founder Sir Stamford Raffles.

Well done! City founder, Sir Stamford Raffles

Singapore makes its money in the bank towers on the other side. The city's most beautiful museums, the large hotels and most exquisite shops are all located in the Colonial Quarter between Chinatown, Little India and the Central Business Districts. This is also where you will see many of the monuments from the days of British colonial rule.

The city fathers, however, have shown courage in combining the new with the old: the old City Hall, in which the Japanese signed the declaration of surrender, and the Supreme Court behind it now form an outstanding museum for south-east Asian art. The new building is graced by a cupola by star architect Sir Norman Foster. The city has also set a sign for its future in its very centre: Singapore has established the green campus of its Management University here. The impressive building of the Art University SOTA with its hanging gardens is located directly opposite.

1 ARMENIAN CHURCH
(136 B1) *(🕮 J4)*

This church, which was built in 1835, is the architect Georg Coleman's masterpiece. The congregation was not completely satisfied with the dome over the nave, however, so in 1850 a spire was planted in its place. Unfortunately, it does not really harmonise with the portico. Many members of what was once a large Armenian community of refugees from Turkey were buried in the cemetery behind the church. The church and cemetery have now been proclaimed national monuments. *60 Hill Street | MRT EW 13, NS 25 City Hall | MRT CC 2 Bras Basah, then bus 197*

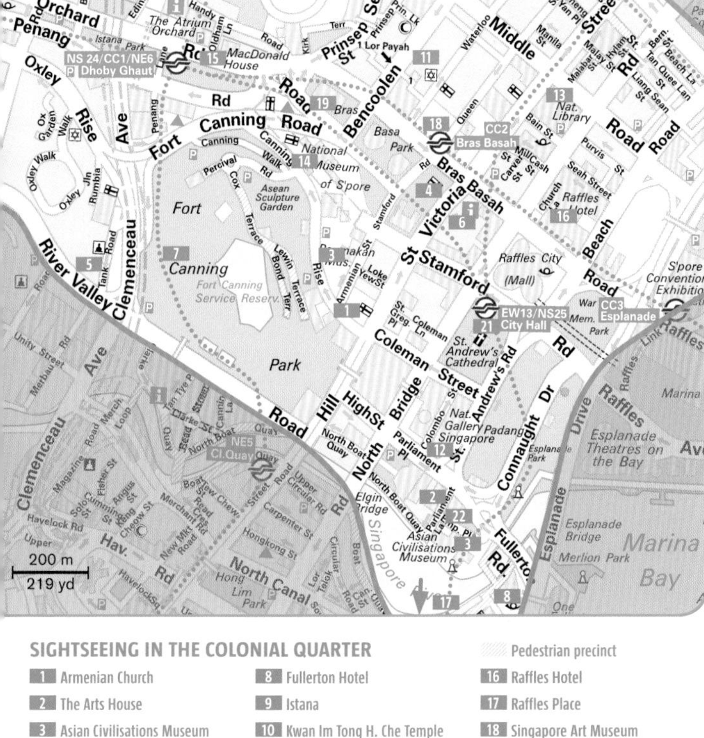

SIGHTSEEING IN THE COLONIAL QUARTER

Pedestrian precinct

1 Armenian Church
2 The Arts House
3 Asian Civilisations Museum
4 Cathedral of the Good Shepherd
5 Chettiars' Temple
6 Chijmes
7 Fort Canning Park
8 Fullerton Hotel
9 Istana
10 Kwan Im Tong H. Che Temple
11 Maghain Aboth Synagogue
12 National Gallery Singapore
13 National Library
14 National Museum of Singapore
15 Orchard Road
16 Raffles Hotel
17 Raffles Place
18 Singapore Art Museum
19 Singapore Management University
20 Sri Krishnan Temple
21 St Andrew's Cathedral
22 Victoria Theatre & Concert Hall

2 THE ARTS HOUSE

(136 B2) (*J4*)

The white building in the heart of the city on the Singapore River has a chequered history: built in 1829 by Irish architect George Coleman as a merchant's residence, it was later re-designated a law court.

Then parliament moved in. It seems only logical that, as a symbol of Singapore's desired transformation into an art capital, the former Old Parliament House was re-named *The Arts House* in 2004 and re-opened as a gallery and event centre with restaurant. Parliament had previously moved a few hundred yards up river to a new building. *1 Old Parliament Lane/corner of High Street | MRT EW 13, NS 25 City Hall | www.theartshouse.com.sg*

3 ASIAN CIVILISATIONS MUSEUM ★ (127 D2–3, 127 D1) (*G4, G3*)

The departments of this museum are contained in two buildings. The main building opposite the Boat Quay concentrates on the cultures of South-East Asia, China, South Asia and Islam. The 135-year-old building is an eye-opener itself and was used by government officials until 2003.

On Armeinian Street at the *Peranakan Museum* (136 B1) (*J3*) (*daily 10am–7pm, Fri until 9pm | admission 6 S$ | 39 Armenian Street | MRT EW 13, NS 25 City Hall | www.peranakanmuseum.org.sg*) visitors can discover the world of the *Peranakan*. These are descendants of the early Chinese immigrants from Malaysia and Singapore. The settlers married women from Malaya (the former name of Malaysia) and even took on some of the customs of the British colonial masters to create a totally unique and new mixed culture. A short film introduces the subject before you enter into the extensive exhibition in the building that was constructed as a schoolhouse in 1910. *Daily 10am–7pm, Fri until 9pm, daily guided tours | free admission | 1 Empress Place | opposite Fullerton Hotel | MRT EW 14, NS 26 Raffles Place | www.acm.org.sg*

LOW BUDGET

Dare to step out onto the *Skybridge (daily 9am–9pm)* on the 50th floor of the *Pinnacle@Duxton* **(135 E–F5) (*H6*)**, a flagship social housing complex in the heart of Chinatown. From up here you get a fabulous view of the city for 5 $S on your Ez-link Card. Entrance procedure under *www.pinnacleduxton.com.sg*

An evening stroll under the old trees at the Asian Civilizations Museum and across the Cavenagh Bridge to the brilliantly illuminated Fullerton Hotel is romantic and free of charge. Things are a little louder on the other side of the Singapore River, but here you will have the lovely path almost to yourself after night falls.

4 CATHEDRAL OF THE GOOD SHEPHERD (136 B1) (*J3*)

The foundation stone for the episcopal see in Singapore was laid in 1843. Its clear lines were designed by J. T. Thompson, a prominent master builder in his day. *Queen Street | MRT EW 13, NS 25 City Hall, MRT CC 2 Bras Basah*

5 CHETTIARS' TEMPLE (SRI THENDAYUTHAPANI TEMPLE) (135 F1) (*H3*)

A temple built on this site in 1850 had to make way for today's building in 1984. The roof is constructed in a manner that makes it possible for the light of morning and evening sun to flow in through 48 decorated panes of glass and fall onto the inner courtyard and altars. The *Chettiars*, who built the temple, were the traditional money-changers whose predecessors came from Madras in South India. The Hindu Thaipusam and Navarathri festivals take place in this temple. *15 Tank Road | MRT CC 1, NE 6, NS 24 Dhoby Ghaut, then bus 64*

6 CHIJMES (136 C1) (*J3*)

The 'j' makes the name of this former convent appear a little unusual but it is simply pronounced *chimes*. The full name was the 'Convent of the Sisters of the Holy Infant Jesus' or CHIJ for short; that explains the 'j'. The buildings themselves are the actual attraction and have been restored to house galleries, restaurants, cafés and boutiques. *Daily 8am–midnight (shops daily 11am–10pm) | free admission | 30 Victoria Street/Bras Basah Road | MRT CC 2 Bras Basah, MRT EW 13, NS 25 City Hall*

7 FORT CANNING PARK
(136 A–B 1–2) (*H–J 3–4*)

You will be able to get a breath of fresh air here only five minutes away from Orchard Road. Delightful Fort Canning Hill provides a good overview of Singapore's history and modern culture. This is where the annual *Womad* music festival is held and *Ballet under the Stars* is performed several times a year. The hill is the oldest royal residence on the island and people lived here 600 years ago: this is the site of the *Keramat* where it is said that Sultan Iskandar Shah was buried. The founder of Singapore, Sir Stamford Raffles, built his first residence on the hill – it has now been reconstructed. There are also some graves of early settlers up here. You will discover the name of George Coleman on one of them; he was the architect of the old Parliament Building and Armenian Church.

The colonial *Fort Canning Centre* with the *Pinacothèque de Paris (Sun–Thu 10am–7.30pm, Fri/Sat 10am–8.30pm | www.pinacotheque.com.sg)* stands above the Keramat. Visitors can take part in an informative tour through the enchanting spice garden *(heritage trail with spice garden | www.nparks.gov.sg)* of the former Botanic Gardens.

The *Hotel Fort Canning* with the adjacent *The Legends Fort Canning Park* are on the other side of the hill. *The Legends* is a private club in a historic building from 1926 with some restaurants open to the public. This once served as the British command headquarters for the Malay Peninsula. *MRT CC 1, NE 6, NS 24 Dhoby Ghaut, then approx. 10 min walk*

Sultans and settlers found their last resting place under the old trees in Fort Canning Park

8 FULLERTON HOTEL
(136 C3) (*J5*)

This grand hotel makes no secret of the fact that £250 million (400 million US$) were spent on its renovation. Singaporeans and tourists alike love to sit on the terrace and look down at the river. A fortress was built at this strategically favourable location in 1829 and named after the first governor Sir Robert Fullerton. The Fullerton Building was erected in 1928 as the main post office. *1 Fullerton Square | MRT EW 14, NS 26 Raffles Place*

9 ISTANA (130 A4) (*H1*)

The Istana – Malay for palace – was once the residence of the representative of the British crown and is now the official address of the President of Singapore. The magnificent building, located in the centre of an enormous park (the entrance is on Orchard Road), is only open to Singaporeans and tourists five times a year: on 1st of January and 1st of May, as well as Chinese New Year, *Hari Raya Puasa* and *Deepavali*. *Orchard Road | MRT CC 1, NE 6, NS 24 Dhoby Ghaut*

10 INSIDER TIP YKWAN IM TONG HOOD CHE TEMPLE
(131 D5) (*J2*)

Although the interior decoration of this modern Buddhist temple cannot be compared with that found in more traditional buildings, visitors will still have plenty to see. The faithful quickly put down their shopping bags and take up bundles of joss sticks that they then reverently hold in their hands. They kneel or sit in prayer in front of the statues of Buddha. Many of them use so-called 'fortune-telling sticks' in their attempts to get an idea of what the future holds in store for them. It is strictly forbidden to take photos inside the temple. *178 Waterloo Street | MRT EW 12 Bugis*

11 MAGHAIN ABOTH SYNAGOGUE
(130 C6) (*J3*)

Arab Jews laid the foundation stone of this house of worship more than 100 years ago making it the oldest seat of the Jewish community in all of South-East Asia. Most of the community came from Baghdad, and from China after the Communists took over control of the country. *24/26 Waterloo Street | MRT CC 1, NE 6, NS 24 Dhoby Ghaut*

12 NATIONAL GALLERY SINGAPORE ★ (136 B2) (*J4*)

A further highlight of the transformation of colonial buildings into modern architecture: at a cost of over half a billion dollars, the city state gutted its former City Hall and Supreme Court buildings. Now joined together, they offer over 645,000 historic square feet showcasing around 800 works of the overall 8000 pieces of south-east Asian art collected over decades. The most fascinating aspect is that the historic chambers and offices have been preserved. The golden canopy over the entrance extends upwards to the roof rerrace. *Sun–Thu 10am–7pm, Fri/Sat 10am–10pm | admission 20 S$ | 1 Saint Andrew's Road | www.nationalgallery.sg | MRT EW 13, NS 25 City Hall*

13 NATIONAL LIBRARY
(131 D6) (*J–K3*)

The new building of the National Library is much more than just a tower full of books. A great number of Singaporeans – more than 1.9 million – are members of the library, which has a stock of around three million books in Chinese, Malay, Tamil and English. Both the building itself and the views over the city from the upper floors are interesting as are the many different kinds of events held here. *Daily 10am–9pm, except public holidays | 100*

Superlative shopping: the shops and malls on Orchard Road are spectacular

Victoria Street | www.nl.sg | MRT EW 12 Bugis, then bus 851

14 NATIONAL MUSEUM OF SINGAPORE (130 C6) (*🕮 J3*)

Singapore's oldest and largest museum was reopened in 2006 after extensive renovations had been completed. It hosts touring exhibitions of an international standard and provides an overview of specific aspects of Singaporean history, such as fashion and food in the city, on almost 20,000 m² (215,000 ft²) of ultramodern exhibition space behind its impressive colonial facade. The architectural highlight of the building is its 24 m (79 ft)-wide glass dome, which is also illuminated at night. *Daily 10am–6pm | admission 6 S$ | 93 Stamford Road | www.nationalmuseum.sg | MRT CC 2 Bras Basah | MRT CC 1, NE 6, NS 24 Dhoby Ghaut*

15 ORCHARD ROAD ★ (129 D–F 4–5) (*🕮 E–H 1–3*)

Singapore's 'Champs Élysées' can now satisfy the most demanding wishes: the shopping street Orchard Road sells everything the world has to offer. Occasionally on Saturday evenings Orchard Road is closed to traffic – and is then packed with hundreds of thousands of people. The consumers' paradise also includes *Tanglin Road*, which enters into Orchard Road, and Scotts Road, which crosses the main shopping street. There are some expensive antique shops in the *Tanglin Shopping Centre*, the second-oldest in the city.

The highlight of Orchard Road is the *ION Orchard* at the junction with Scotts Road. There are 335 shops on the 59,000 m² (635,000 ft²) of floor space. Shoppers can choose between Adidas and Yves Saint-Laurent, between Italian ice cream and Ice

Kachang – frozen water with syrup. The Singaporeans are particularly fond of *313@ Somerset* with eight floors of shops such as Zara and Uniqlo. There are also excellent *food courts* on the top floor. *Orchard Central* (Desigual, Dean & Deluca) and *Orchard Gateway* together make up the huge 313@ Somerset shopping complex.

Ngee Anm City, with the Japanese *Takashimaya* department store, offers a wide range of shops. There are regular bargain markets for toys, sporting equipment and other goods in the basement.

The Paragon on the other side of the road is the place to go for elegant fashion from companies such as Banana Republic and Muji from Japan. Young people are magically drawn to the trendy *The Cathay* at the bottom of Orchard Road. The renovated *The Heeren* is home to a branch of the traditional Robinsons department store, offering brands such as Shinola from Detroit. The large shopping malls are open from 10am to 10pm. *MRT NS 22 Orchard, NS 23 Somerset*

16 RAFFLES HOTEL ★

(136 C1) (*Ⓜ K3*)

The 'Grand Old Lady of the East' has emerged from the fountain of youth but the legend is just as alive as it ever was. It began in 1887 when the three Armenian Sarkies brothers rented a house directly on the beach promenade and converted it into a hotel. The Sarkies, who named their hotel after Sir Stamford Raffles, rebuilt and expanded until Raffles became the top address in town. Emperors, kings and presidents, heads of state and stars have all lived in Raffles. Writers and journalist from all over the world used to meet in the *Writers Bar* to sip the *Singapore Sling* – a cocktail of gin and exotic fruit juices that really packs a punch. This period was interrupted by the Second World War when the hotel was turned into quarters for the Japanese occupiers. After the war, Raffles was able to pick up the thread of the glorious old days once again but in the 1980s it was only living from its old reputation. Instead of tearing it down,

OPEN-AIR ART

Salvador Dalí, Henry Moore, Roy Lichtenstein and Fernando Botero are probably the most famous international artists whose works can be admired outdoors in Singapore. In addition, dozens of sculptures by Asian artists have been installed throughout the city. You will soon come across Dalí's *Homage to Newton* and Botero's *Bird* as you stroll along the Singapore River; the enormous bird created by Botero squats prominently on the Quay. There, you will also find figures such as the children jumping into the river by the famous Singaporean artist Chong Fah Cheong, symbolising old and new life in the city. Roy Lichtenstein's gigantic *Six Brushstrokes* adorns and enriches a skyscraper in the Suntec commercial area. That is also the location of what is supposedly the largest fountain in the world – the *Fountain of Wealth* created by Calvin Tsao and Zack Mckown. Visitors will mainly find works by Asian artists in the Vivo City business area near the harbour. The centre acquired some of the sculptures shown during Singapore's Biennale. The tourist office can provide a leaflet with details of recommended cultural walks.

Where banks soar skywards: Raffles Place financial centre

Singapore completely renovated its gem and the rejuvenated old house has greeted its guests in dazzling white since 1991. Walk up the gravel driveway to the elaborate wrought-iron portico, have a look inside the enormous hotel hall, see if you can still find traces of Somerset Maugham, Hermann Hesse and Noel Coward in the Writers Bar. The attractive inner courtyards, tropical garden, six restaurants, several dozen high-class shops, a theatre and ballroom are all open to the general public. *Sandals, shorts and sleeveless shirts are not deemed appropriate in the hotel | 1 Beach Road | MRT CC 2 Bras Basah*

17 RAFFLES PLACE

(136 B3) (*J5*)

You can feel the heartbeat of the financial metropolis around Raffles Place. The core of Singapore's Central Business District is surrounded by a ring of high-rise towers belonging to the banks. If you take Exit B out of the underground station, you will see Caltex House on your left with the Bank of China, built in a classical modern style, further to the left. Today, its 18 storeys seem rather insignificant, and it is almost overpowered by the gigantic Maybank Building on the right. The two towers housing the offices of the United Overseas Bank next to the sweeping Standard Chartered Bank Building resemble a stack of coins on top of each other. *MRT EW 14, NS 26 Raffles Place*

18 SINGAPORE ART MUSEUM ●

(130) C6) (*J3*)

The building, which once housed St Joseph's Institution, the first Catholic school in Singapore, has been lavishly renovated and now serves as the National Gallery. The permanent collection is made up of 5500 exhibits focusing on contemporary South-East Asian art. *Daily 10am–7pm, Fri to 9pm | admission 10 S$, Fri from 6pm free admission | 71 Bras Basah Road | MRT CC 2 Bras Basah*

19 SINGAPORE MANAGEMENT UNIVERSITY (130 C6) (J3)

This building is not a university but a declaration – a declaration of the city's desire to be an academic centre, and that is one of the reasons that the SMU Building was erected between historical buildings in the very heart of the city. The third university in the five-million metropolis is closely modelled on American institutions of this kind and attracts students from all over the world. Anybody who wants to experience the feeling of young Singapore and its desire to learn should not hesitate to visit the open campus or the passages in the basement. *81 Victoria Street | www.smu.edu.sg | MRT CC 2 Bras Basah*

20 INSIDER TIP SRI KRISHNAN TEMPLE (131 D5) (J2)

The vibrant colours are the most fascinating attribute of this Hindu temple. Ceremonies are held in the midst of the hustle and bustle of everyday life; quite often accompanied by music. The various gods – usually Shiva, Vishnu and Brahma – shown in the past, present and future are decorated with fresh flowers. It is a bit strange that Buddhists from the neighbouring *Kwan Im Tong Hood Che Temple* often drop in to pay their respects to the Hindu deities. *152 Waterloo Street | MRT EW 12 Bugis*

Offer flowers to the gods and pause for a moment in the daily rush: Hindu temple Sri Krishnan

21 ST ANDREW'S CATHEDRAL (136 B–C1) (J4)

This neo-Gothic Anglican church was built by Indian prisoners in 1862. The dazzling white of the facade and tower are the result of a unique mixture known as Madras

Churam that was used for the plastering: shells, egg white and coconut fibres were stirred into it. *11 St Andrew's Road | MRT EW 13, NS 25 City Hall*

22 VICTORIA THEATRE AND CONCERT HALL (136 B2) (J4)

A huge amount of time and money was invested in renovating Singapore's traditional *Victoria Concert Hall* in 2014. The façades remained intact, while the interior was given state-of-the-art acoustics. The clock mechanism in the bell tower was restored by the same British company which built it at the beginning of the 20th century. The old chairs were used to create the ceiling of the bar; elements of the armrests provide sound insulation. Both halls serve as prime examples of Singapore's new approach to preserving the old and harmonising with the new. *Daily 10am–9pm | 11 Empress Place | www.vtvch.com | MRT EW 13, NS 25 City Hall*

MARINA BAY

One of Singapore's many unique qualities is its ability to invent itself anew time and time again. The government feels that this is the only way the tiny city state will be able to remain 'relevant'. The district around Marina Bay is the symbol of this rebirth.

This was once the mouth of the Singapore River but now the artificial bay is the largest fresh-water reservoir in the city, and Singapore is no longer dependent on being supplied with water from its neighbouring country Malaysia. The lake is also a paradise for water sports enthusiasts – this is where motorboat races and sailing regattas are held; there are fountains and ship parades. But, first and foremost, Marina Bay is where tourists are offered an almost unbelievable number of attractions in a very small area. It is only a stone's throw away from the Business District, the streets around Shenton Way and the Boat Quay promenade. Marina Bay is also only a short walk away from the Colonial Quarter. The *Suntec City* commercial centre to the north of the bay is also part of this development. This shopping area, which was designed as a city within the city, is flanked by the towers of five office buildings (number five is smaller than the others).

Marina Bay is dominated by the three gigantic towers of the *Marina Bay Sands Hotel*, MBS for short. An enormous rooftop terrace spans the trio of towers at a height of 200 m (656 ft) above the ground; its top is open to visitors. The panoramic view from here reaches as far as the Indonesian island of Sumatra and to Malaysia. In the meantime, the MBS has become the most photographed building in Singapore and probably in all of South-East Asia.

The chic casino, the 'Louis Vuitton Island', as well as congress centres and restaurants are located beneath the towers. Right next door is the newly created Botanic Gardens, the *Gardens by the Bay* and, opposite, there is the popular *Singapore Flyer* – a giant observation wheel. This new city district was established on new land wrested from the sea.

1 ART SCIENCE MUSEUM (137 D3) (K5)

From the outside, this futuristic construction looks like a gigantic lotus blossom while the architecture creates fascinating spaces in the interior. Some of the world's best exhibitions are shown here – from a Da-Vinci retrospective to a show about the sinking of the Titanic. *Daily 10am–7pm | admission 15–25 S$, depending on the exhibition; combined ticket for all exhibitions 28 S$, Fri is family day:*

2 children get in free on an adult ticket | 10 Bayfront Av. | ticket hotline tel. 66 88 88 26 | www.marinabaysands.com | MRT CE 2, NS 27 Marina Bay | MRT CC 4 Promenade | MRT CE 1 DT

2 ESPLANADE
(136 C2) (*⌧ K4*)

Singapore's Esplanade complex on the northern edge of Marina Bay includes a 2000-seat theatre, a concert hall for an audience of 1600 and a shopping centre. The architecture has polarised many Singaporeans: while the building's fans are wild about its appearance, those less enamoured lambaste the design of the glass roof with its spiky protective construction. This has led to its nickname: it is now known as the *durian* because it looks like the prickly skin of the South-East Asians' favourite fruit. It is really delicious but the smell is so pungent that it is forbidden to eat it on buses and trains. *1 Raffles Av. | www.esplanade.com | MRT EW 14, NS 26 Raffles Place, MRT EW 13, NS 25 City Hall | MRT CC 3 Esplanade*

3 GARDENS BY THE BAY ★
(137 E–F 2–4) (*⌧ L–M 4–6*)

The second large botanical garden in this tropical city was opened in 2012; it is enormous, just like everything else created here. The Gardens by the Bay cover an area of around 247 acres, making them half the size of Monaco. The gardens are spread over three strips of land around Marina Bay. *Bay South* – actually the new botanical garden – covers an area of 54 ha (133 ac) itself. There is an open-air arena for 30,000 spectators in the com-

One of the new symbols of Marina Bay: the lotus blossom of the Art Science Museum

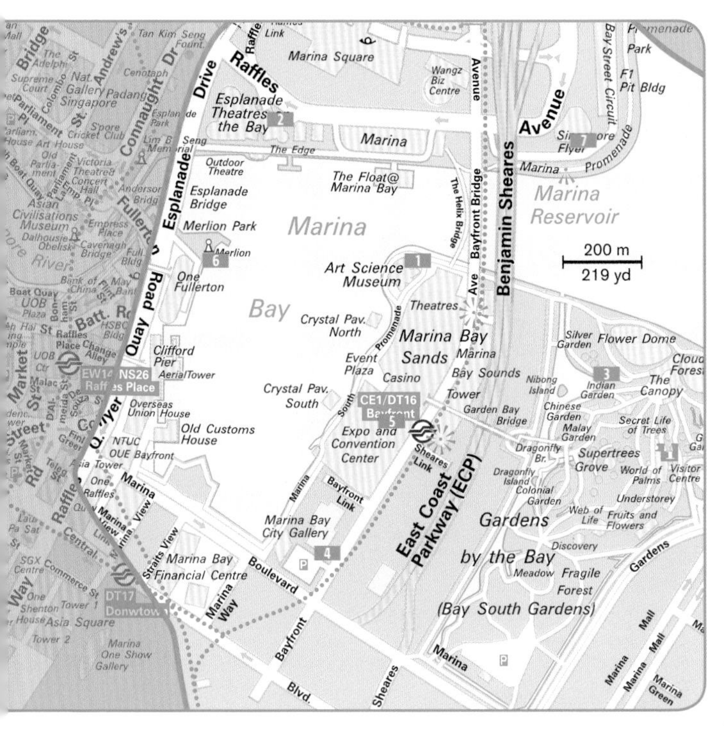

SIGHTSEEING IN MARINA BAY

- **1** Art Science Museum
- **2** Esplanade
- **3** Gardens by the Bay
- **4** Marina Bay City Gallery
- **5** Marina Bay Sands
- Pedestrian precinct
- **6** Merlion Park & Fullerton Complex
- **7** Singapore Flyer & Formula 1

plex. Visitors can satisfy their hunger in 13 restaurants, one of which, the *Pollen* in the Flower Dome, is run by London star chefJason Atherton. The planners are counting on around five million visitors annually – that equals the number of people living in the city. This might actually be the case because nothing is too exclusive for these gardens. The garden architects, for instance, paid 30,000 S$ for a 500-year-old camellia that they found in China. The ● greenhouses, *Flower Dome* and *Cloud Forest*, located in two domed buildings, offer people living in the tropics an opportunity to admire the vegetation of the cooler areas of the earth. The lofty artificial tropical trees made of steel are useful attractions: they serve as exhaust ducts for the air-conditioning, which is fuelled with green waste. The restaurant *Supertree by Indochine* is in the highest of these *super trees* The new terminal for cruise ships has been established directly behind the garden. The main building of the *Marina Barrage (Sun–Mon 9am–9pm | free admission | 8 Marina Gardens Drive | www.pub.gov.sg | MRT CE 2 Marina Bay, then bus 400)*, a barrier to

Pools with wow factor: the Skypark on the three towers of the Marina Bay Sands Hotel

a gigantic fresh-water reservoir, on the bay side has a lovely rooftop terrace and an educational centre for Singapore's water resources management. At weekends Chinese fly their kites from the terrace. *Daily 9am–9pm | admission 28 S$ | 18 Marina Gardens Drive | www.gardensbythebay.com | MRT DT 16, CE 1 Bayfront | MRT NS 27 Marina Bay*

4 MARINA BAY CITY GALLERY
(136141 C–D4) *(K6)*

When looking at the water from the Marina Bay Sands Complex, the visitor centre is located in a pavilion on the left. Here you will find a large model of the entire new city. This is also where guided tours start and where you can obtain flyers with recommendations for sightseeing routes, such as the *Architecture Trail*, around the bay. If you need refreshments, you only have to walk a few yards to the escalator that takes you to the *Marina Bay Link Mall* where there are some bakeries and charming delicatessens such as *Ichiban Boshi (B2–14/15)* or *The Soup Spoon (B2–41)*. *Tue–Sun 10am–8pm | free admission | 11 Marina Blvd. | www.marinabay.sg | MRT CE 1, DT 16 Bayfront*

5 MARINA BAY SANDS ★
(137 D3–4) *(K–L5)*

This gigantic complex is actually a city in its own right with a hotel, 50 restaurants, the casino, a musical theatre and a skating rink made of plastic. Above the ground, it is dominated by the MBS Hotel with its 2560 rooms *(www.marinabaysands.com)* and the congress centre opposite it. There is even a 146-m (160-yd)-long pool on the roof, which is unfortunately reserved for hotel guests. The express lift whisks visitors up to the Skypark *(Mon–Thu 9.30am–10pm, Fri–Sun 9.30am–11pm | 23 S$, tickets at the site, at tel. 66 88 88 26 | www.marinabaysands.com)* on the rooftop terrace in a mere 19 seconds.

Underground, you will be amazed by the sheer extent of the shopping area, which is full of luxury boutiques and has a very good food court at the end.
In the cellar, Indonesian gondoliers will row you along a canal that ends underneath an enormous water funnel. Rain gushes into the funnel during tropical downpours and produces a magnificent spectacle that is intended to symbolize increasing wealth. There is also sufficient space in the basement for Singapore's largest casino that boasts more than 650 gaming tables. Foreigners do not have to pay an admission fee.
It is also well worth making a visit to the flagship store of the luxury luggage brand, Louis Vuitton, which is located on an island in the bay. You can reach it via a tunnel or over an outdoor bridge. The night flies by in the two-storey entertainment complex's disco, *Avalon (Wed, Fri–Sun from 10pm | admission Wed, Fri, Sun 30, Sat 35 S$)* and at the *Pangaea (Thu–Sat from 10pm | admission 40 S$)* lounge. In the evening, the MBS waterfront becomes the projection surface for a magical display of lights *(15-minute laser show Wonder Full Sun–Thu 8 and 9.30pm, Fri/Sat 8, 9.30 and 11pm). MRT CE 1 DT 16 Bayfront*

6 MERLION PARK & FULLERTON HERITAGE (136 C3–4) (*J–K 4–5*)

Prince Nila Utama named the small piece of land he discovered in the late 13th century *Singa Pura* after a mythical beast – half fish and half lion – the prince is said to have spotted in the dense rainforest. Singapore has taken on the Merlion as its symbol. The 8.6m (28ft)-high statue at the end of the One Fullerton restaurant complex spouts water into the sea. Try not to get mixed up with all of the 'Fullertons' here: not only the impressive hotel in the Colonial Quarter is named after him, the entire region has Robert Fullerton, the first governor of the Straits Settlements, the British crown colony consisting of Penang, Malacca and Singapore, to thank for its name. The Fullerton Waterboat House is behind One Fullerton; if you walk along the water, you will soon reach the new restaurant district around the *Fullerton Bay Hotel (www.fullertonbayhotel.com)*; this is one of Singapore's most beautiful luxury hotels. In the delightfully restored arrivals hall of the adjacent Clifford Pier *The Clifford Pier* restaurant serves up Asian specialities.
The *Lantern* rooftop terrace of the *Fullerton Bay Hotel* is considered one of the loveliest places in Singapore to wel-

NEW LAND

In recent years, Singapore has reclaimed land from the sea – so far, almost 46 mi² – and the city has increased in size from 580 km² (223 mi²) to 697 km² (269 mi²), with 760 km² (293 mi²) as the long-term target. As just one example, Singapore's modern Changi Airport stands on reclaimed land. Tekong Island in the north-east is presently being expanded. The banking district is built on sand fill, as is the new business city that is now being constructed around the harbour. The land is won by piling up sand – sand, that the island-state has to buy expensively in Indonesia. By the way, the coastline once ran along Beach Road.

come the evening. There are several smaller restaurants behind it in the *Customs House*. *MRT EW 14, NS 26 Raffles Place*

A leisurely revolution: Singapore Flyer

7 SINGAPORE FLYER & FORMULA 1 (O) (🕮 J4)

Leaving the Marina Bay Sands complex over the Helix Bridge (137 D2–3) (🕮 L4–5), you soon reach the Singapore Flyer, an observation wheel, on the right-hand side. In spite of some turmoil concerning its financing, it turns quite happily. Even though it may not seem like it, the Singapore Flyer revolves twenty-four hours a day – but very slowly. It was built by a German businessman, who admittedly, together with the banks, relieved his investors of their money. For a time he was not allowed to leave Singapore. The building with the box stops for the Formula 1 races is behind the observation wheel. The Singapore Grand Prix held every autumn is the first ever night-time event in Formula 1 racing. *Singapore Flyer daily 8.30am–10.30pm | 30-minute ride 33 S$, many special prices | 30 Raffles Av. | www.singaporeflyer.com | MRT CC 4 Promenade*

CHINATOWN & SINGAPORE RIVER

Anybody who just thinks of Chinatown as another tourist attraction will miss out on all its enigmatic aspects. Make sure that you have enough time to explore the hidden lanes in this area instead of just strolling up and down in the overcrowded pedestrian precinct.

Visit the temples here; by the way, they are not all of Chinese origin. This district is particularly interesting at Chinese New Year, which is celebrated in January or February. Weeks before the event, the entire district is transformed into a market with hawkers and red lanterns glowing everywhere in the evening.

You can also eat well here, although the prices are not always reasonable. Chinatown is a good place to buy souvenirs. You can have a Chinese merchant weigh out tea for you to take home, for instance, or inhale the aroma of dried seahorses and lizards in a traditional chemist's shop. There are interesting museums dealing with the history of Chinatown and the future of the city here. At the end of the day, quite a few bottles of champagne get uncorked in the bars around Club Street and Duxton Road. If you are looking for

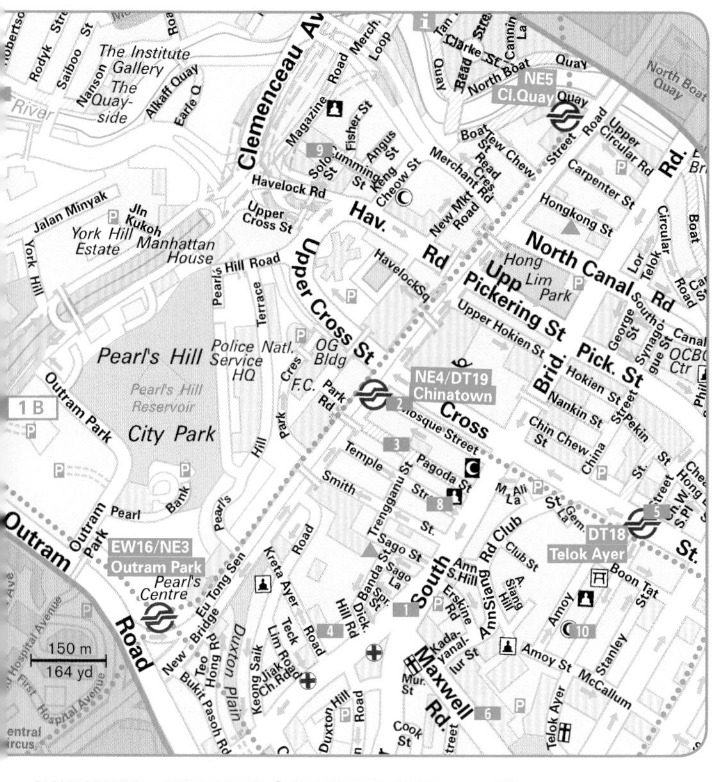

SIGHTSEEING – CHINATOWN & SINGAPORE RIVER

1 Buddha Tooth Relic Temple
2 Chinatown
3 Chinatown Heritage Centre
4 Chinatown Visitor Centre
5 Fuk Tak Ch'i Museum/ Far East Square
6 Singapore City Gallery (URA)
7 Singapore Tyler Print Institute
8 Sri Mariamman Temple
9 Tan Si Chong Su Temple
10 Thian Hock Keng Temple
Pedestrian precinct

something more relaxed, stroll across to the Singapore River. One side exudes a romantic atmosphere. In the early evening, people walk past the magnificently restored colonial buildings in the shade of the old trees. On the other side and along the upper reaches of the river, you will find the best pubs and bars in town. The nightlife here on Clarke Quay is boisterous, it is loud and fun, it is the perfect place to see and be seen.

1 BUDDHA TOOTH RELIC TEMPLE
(136 A4) (*H5*)

There are many old temples in Chinatown – and one new one in the very centre. For this temple intended to house Buddha's tooth, the architect took his inspiration for the design from the mandala – the symbol of the Buddhist universe. Unfortunately, soon after it was consecrated in 2007, it was discovered that the tooth most probably came from a cow. And that after the Singaporeans had donated more than £20 million (33 million US$) and a good 440 lbs (200 kg) of gold for its construction. *288 South Bridge Road | www.btrts.org.sg | MRT EW 15 Tanjong Pagar*

2 CHINATOWN ★ ●
(135 E–F 2–5) *(🕮 H–J 4–6)*

Chinatown was the birthplace of Singapore as an important trading centre. The government has invested £40 million (65 million US$) in the restoration of the houses here that had been at risk of being demolished. It is well worth visiting the area between Pickering Street/Church Street in the north, Telok Ayer Street/Anson Road in the east, Cantonment Road in the south and New Bridge Road in the west – both to admire the architectural fabric that has been preserved and, in particular, to see the typical shops and their owners. The original houses in Chinatown are a reminder of the luxury merchants once lived in and the power of the Chinese clans. The architecture is a mixture of Chinese elements and Doric and Corinthian columns with a dash of Classicism from Italy; the final result is now known as 'Chinese Baroque'. *MRT NE 4, DT 19 Chinatown*

3 CHINATOWN HERITAGE CENTRE
(136 A3) *(🕮 H5))*

Essentially, this museum depicts the often hard, but also colourful life of the Chinese in Singapore, presented in painstakingly renovated, former shophouses. At the same time, numerous interactive exhibits explain the history of the Chinese exiles, the formation of the clans and also Chinatown's most recent developments. A must for those who want to understand the Singapore of the Chinese. *Daily 9am–8pm, closed 1st Mon in month | admission 15 S$ | 48 Pagoda Street | www.chinatownheritagecentre.com.sg | MRT NE 4 Chinatown*

4 CHINATOWN VISITOR CENTRE
(135 E4) *(🕮 H5)*

This centre was established on the initiative of the business people in Chinatown and sells articles hand-made by elderly citizens. A third of the proceeds is given to the seamstresses. An exhibition provides information about Chinatown and its his-

RELAX & ENJOY

Singapore is perfect if you want to pamper yourself – the possibilities are enormous. Painted nails are a must, especially if you decide to wear flip-flops. The specialists at *Snails Beauty* **(129 D4)** ***(🕮 F2)***, centrally located with a view of Orchard Road, work quickly and professionally – you could hardly ask for more *(501 Orchard Road, #03-01 Wheelock Place | tel. 67 38 01 00 | MRT NS 22 Orchard)*. The ● *Beauty Emporium at House (8d Dempsey Road)* **(0)** ***(🕮 B2)*** offers everything to do with beauty. Its own *Spa Esprit (daily 10am–10pm | #02–01 | tel. 64 75 73 75 | www.spa-esprit.com)* rates as one of the best in the city. The *Willow Stream Spa* **(136 C1)** ***(🕮 J3)*** *(Hotel Fairmont Singapore | 80 Bras Basah Road | tel. 63 39 77 77 | www.willowstream.com | MRT CC 2 Bras Basah)* is one of the most luxurious day spas; it even offers a special *Shoppers Relief Massage* to take care of its clients' special needs.

Typical Chinatown: colourful mix of shophouses, modern architecture and old symbols

tory. You can also book tours through Chinatown here (p. 124). *Mon–Fri 9am–9pm, Sat/Sun 9am–10pm | 2 Banda Street | at Kreta Ayer Square, next to the Buddha Tooth Relic Temple | MRT NE 4 Chinatown*

5 INSIDER TIP FUK TAK CH'I MUSEUM/FAR EAST SQUARE (136 B4) (*🕮 J5*)

A small museum was opened in Singapore's oldest temple, Fuk Tak Ch'i, giving an insight into the everyday life of the first Chinese immigrants. The museum is part of Far East Square, a former residential district between Telok Ayer, Pekin, China and Cross Streets. Part of the area was restored at the end of the 1990s and covered with a glass roof. You can stroll the air-conditioned streets and look at the traditional shophouses, stop off at one of the restaurants and cafés and buy souvenirs. Cultural events are now held in a pavilion on the site of past Chinese street-opera performances. *Daily 10am–10pm | free admission | 76 Telok Ayer Street/Far East Square | MRT NE 4 Chinatown*

6 INSIDER TIP SINGAPORE CITY GALLERY (URA) (136 A4–5) (*🕮 H6*)

This is the place for anybody who is interested in Singapore's city planning and architecture: the two-floor gallery in the building of the Urban Redevelopment Authority (URA) hosts thematic exhibitions such as the restoration activities in Little India and has two gigantic models of the city with plans for its development over the coming decades. Interactive screens and 3D animations create a visual image of the new Singapore. *Mon–Fri 9am–5pm | free admission | 45 Maxwell Road | www.ura.gov.sg | MRT EW 15 Tanjong Pagar*

7 SINGAPORE TYLER PRINT INSTITUTE (126 A2) (*🕮 E4*)

As a symbol of Singapore's new focus on art, the city went to great efforts to bring a branch of the famous New York printing shop to the tropical island. Inspired by the American master printer Kenneth Tyler, the institute displays modern graphic art in its gallery, organises workshops on paper and even has a paper mill. This makes it possible to display the entire process from dipping the paper to the collaboration with artists and printing, as well as selling the artworks. The Singapore Tyler Print Museum also publishes its own edition of books and devotes exhibitions to guest artists. The STPI is located on the upper floor of a renovated harbour warehouse. *Tue–Fri 10am–7pm, Sat 9am–6pm | free admission | 41 Robertson Quay | www.stpi.com.sg | bus 32, 54, 64, 123, 143, 195 Clarke Quay | MRT NE 5 Clarke Quay, then bus 54*

8 SRI MARIAMMAN TEMPLE ★ (136 A4) (*🕮 H5*)

This Hindu sanctuary was founded in 1827. In 1843, the original wooden building was replaced by the current stone construction. Since those days, it has been frequently extended and redecorated. The temple is full of elaborate carvings and sculptures. The *Gopuram*, the entrance door, tells a long story in pictures itself. Weddings are held here almost every day; there is traditional music in the evening and fire-walking takes place in the inner courtyard during the Thimi festival. *244 South Bridge Road | MRT EW 15 Tanjong Pagar, MRT NE 4, DT 19 Chinatown*

9 TAN SI CHONG SU TEMPLE (135 E–F2) (*🕮 H4*)

Singapore's Chinese are absolutely convinced that this sanctuary, building of which was completed in 1876, has the best *feng shui* in the city. It is said that prayers said in this temple have a better chance of being heard than anywhere else in Singapore. That is why you will find a large number of the faithful here during the main prayer times early in the morn-

Sri Mariamman Temple – a Hindu sanctuary in Chinatown? Completely normal in Singapore

ing and in the evening, and you will be able to experience many fascinating rituals including the Tao liturgy and telling the future with fortune-telling sticks. *15 Magazine Road | MRT NE 4, DT 19 Chinatown, then bus 51*

10 THIAN HOCK KENG TEMPLE ★ ●
(136 A4) (🗺 H5)

Chinese seamen had a temple dedicated to their patron saint Mazu erected here on what was once the coastal road in 1842. (Today, it is difficult to believe that the goddess once looked straight out to sea.) Material from all over the world was used in its construction: the statue of the goddess comes from China, the wrought-iron railings from Scotland, the tiles from England and Holland. The walls and columns are decorated with carvings. The faithful light joss sticks in front of the altars and burn slips of paper with their prayers and vows on them. However, the fortune tellers now work with computers! *158 Telok Ayer Street | MRT DT 18 Telok Ayer*

LITTLE INDIA/ ARAB STREET/ KAMPONG GLAM

The Indian district with its little side streets is the most colourful shopping paradise in all of Singapore.

You can find everything the subcontinent has to offer in Little India – but, without any of the local travel risks. The fabric sellers on Arab Street offer Chinese brocade, Thai silk, and batiks from Indonesia and Malaysia, but you must reach an agreement on the price you pay yourself. The adjacent Muslim quarter, Kampong Glam, is the place to buy perfume oils and the magnificent curved daggers that are still used for certain ceremonies today.

The district is dominated by the Sultan Mosque with its golden roof. Next to it, you will not only find the best Muslim restaurants in Singapore but also the *Malay Heritage Centre* in a restored sultan's palace.

A new fashionable district is currently developing around the mosque. Bars and clubs are shooting up with dizzying speed in places where they did not exist six weeks before. Bear in mind that most of the shops here are not only closed on Sunday but also on Friday afternoon. The pavement restaurants open their doors after sunset during the fasting month of Ramadan and there are usually long queues waiting to enjoy all the delicacies they have to offer.

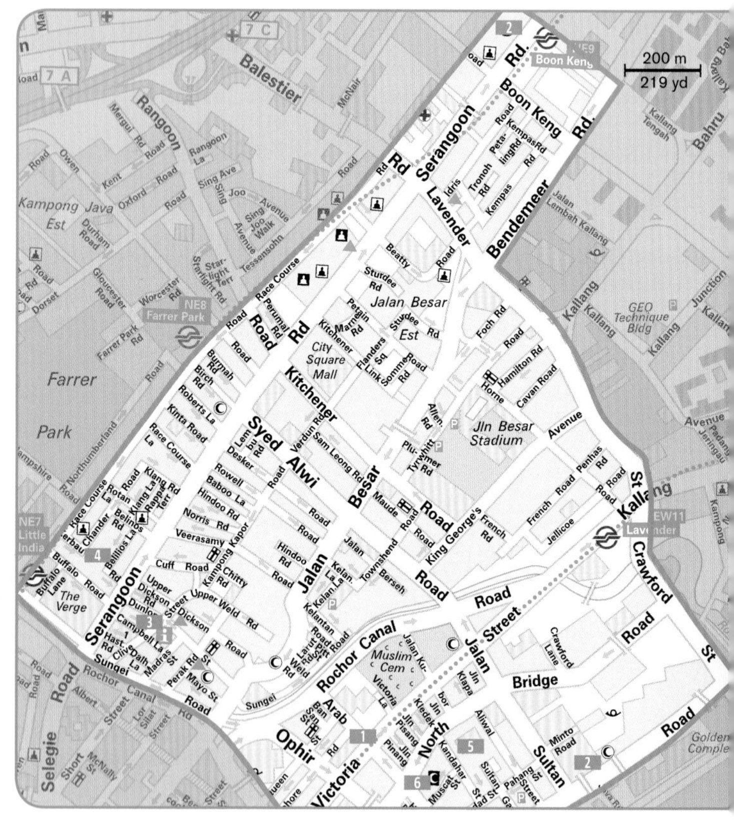

SIGHTSEEING IN LITTLE INDIA & ARAB STREET

Pedestrian precinct

1 Arab Street
2 Hajjah Fatimah Mosque
3 Indian Heritage Centre
4 Little India
5 Malay Heritage Centre
6 Sultan Mosque

1 ARAB STREET (131 D4–E5) (*🕮 K2*)
The Arabs were among the first trade partners of old Singaporea. The street named after them became a synonym for the Malay district that is quite clearly influenced by Islam. The golden dome of the *Sultan Mosque* dominates the area between Jalan Besar and Beach Road in the west and east. The shops in the small streets are full of leather goods and wickerwork, perfume oil, batiks and silk. If you are adept at bargaining, you should be able to get a ten percent discount from the fabric dealers on Arab Street. The high rents in the district, which is also known as *Kampong Glam*, led to many premises remaining empty for long periods but now new life is coming into the area. Singapore's increasingly open in-crowd is now discovering the streets and their attractive nightspots. *MRT EW 12, DT 14 Bugis, then bus 2, 7, 32*

2 HAJJAH FATIMAH MOSQUE
(131 F5) (*🕮 L2*)

The oldest mosque in Singapore is architecturally more beautiful than the larger Sultan Mosque. It was named after a Malay woman born in Malacca who married a wealthy sultan and who was so successful in running his shipping and trading house after his death that she was able to finance construction of this mosque that was opened in 1846. *4001 Beach Road | MRT EW 11 Lavender, then bus 100, 961, 980*

3 INDIAN HERITAGE CENTRE
(130 C4) (*🕮 J2*)

The Indian Heritage Centre gives a good insight into the colourful Indian district and Indian culture. It was opened at the end of 2015 with much pomp behind the exciting and cololurful façade. Even before it got its home, the centre was offering courses, such as 'Cooking with the queen of spices' or 'Indian printing techniques'. Prior to opening, the population was called upon to donate old treasures and photos of Little India in days gone by for the the permanent exhitibion. *Tue–Thu 10am–7pm, Fri/Sat 10am–8pm, Sun 10am–4pm | admission 4 S$ | 5 Campbell Lane | www.indianheritage.org.sg | MRT NE 7 Little India*

4 LITTLE INDIA ★ ●
(130–131 C–E 2–4) (*🕮 J–K 1–2*)

The many women in saris and men in turbans and the traditional lunghi or dhoti

The Sultan Mosque impresses with its sheer size and golden dome

trousers – to be seen on both sides of Serangoon Road as far as Lavender Street in the north and bordering on the Malay district in the east – clearly show that Indians are in the majority in this area. The busiest time here is on Sunday evening when not only the Singaporeans with Indian roots but also many immigrant workers from Bangladesh, Sri Lanka and South India get together on Serangoon Plaza and in front of the Kali Amman Temple. *MRT NE 7 Little India*

5 MALAY HERITAGE CENTRE (131 E5) (*🕮 L2*)

The centre has permanent and temporary exhibitions of Malay art and culture. Situated in a restored sultan's palace, it also offers visitors courses in traditional Malay arts and crafts. Singapore has put a lot of effort into re-appraising the legacy of this ethnic group. *Tue–Sun 10am–6pm, guided tours Tue–Fri 11am | admission 4 S$ | 85 Sultan Gate | www.malayheritage.org.sg | MRT EW 12, DT 14 Bugis, then bus 7*

6 SULTAN MOSQUE (131 E5) (*🕮 K2*)

Construction of the Sultan Mosque as we see it today, crowned with a gigantic golden dome, was only completed in 1928. It is the spiritual centre for Singapore's Muslims and has the largest prayer hall in the city. *No visits during the hours of prayer | 3 Muscat Street | MRT EW 12, DT 14 Bugis*

HARBOURFRONT & SENTOSA

The new harbour district at the gateway to Sentosa, the leisure-time island, is experiencing a period of rapid growth. The Vivo City shopping centre is one of the most beautiful in the city. Nearby, architect Daniel Libeskind built the curved residential towers that look almost as though they are bending in the breeze. You will be over-

Everybody shops in Little India: Muslims, Hindus, Buddhists, Christians, tourists ...

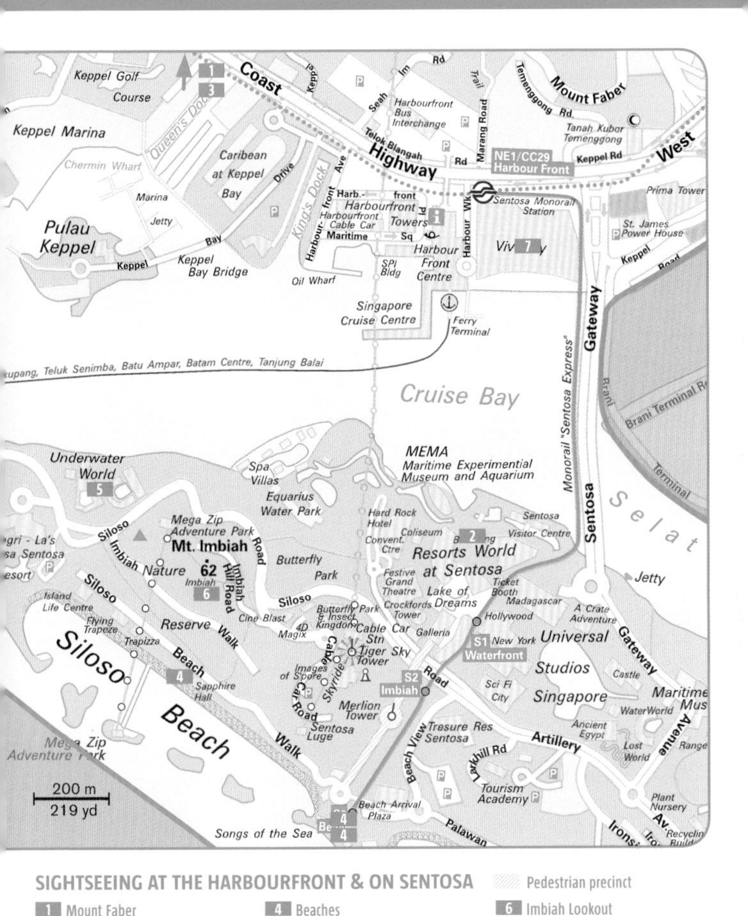

SIGHTSEEING AT THE HARBOURFRONT & ON SENTOSA

1 Mount Faber
2 Resort World Sentosa
3 Southern Ridges
4 Beaches
5 Underwater World
6 Imbiah Lookout Amusement District
7 Vivo City
Pedestrian precinct

whelmed by Sentosa *(sentosa.com.sg)* opposite, especially if you have children with you. The leisure island with its around 250 different attractions is a completely unique world even though it is only a few minutes away from the inner city. Once upon a time, the one-and-a-half-square mile 'Island of Peace and Tranquillity' was only a fishing village. The British started using it as a military base in 1880 to protect Singapore from an attack from the sea – which actually never took place. Today, Sentosa is a paradise for anybody looking for amusement: there are countless attractions around the *Resort World Sentosa* amusement park, high-class restaurants and pizzerias, white beaches and aquariums – you could spend days on Sentosa!
The island is connected to the city by a cable car from Mount Faber (see p. 54).

A bit of Disneyland, a touch of Hollywood, right in the heart of Singapore: Resort World Sentosa

You can reach Sentosa easily by taking the Sentosa Express *(daily 7am–midnight from Vivo City, 3rd floor | admission 4 S$ with Sentosa Pass | MRT CC 29, NE 1 HarbourFront)*, taxi, car or by walking across the new *Sentosa Boardwalk (admission 1 S$, Sat/Sun free)*. There are different prices for taxis and cars ranging from 2–7 S$ per vehicle. The means of transport on Sentosa itself are free; the yellow, red, and blue bus lines and Beach Train head for the various destinations. The island is also ideal for being explored on a *Segway tour (daily 10am–8.30pm and night tours | from 12 S$ starting at Beach Station)* or by electric bicycle *(daily 10am–8pm | from 12 S$ starting at Siloso Beach)*. More about Sentosa on the informative website *www.sentosa.com.sg*.

1 MOUNT FABER
(138 B–C1) *(P4)*

Many visitors begin their excursion to Sentosa at Mount Faber: a cable car runs from there to the island. But, the second-highest mountain in Singapore has much more than just a spectacular view over the city to offer – especially in the evening. The cable car leaves from the *Jewel Box*, which is next to some restaurants and a souvenir shop. *Daily 8.45am–10pm | return ticket 29 S$ incl. admission for Sentosa, many special rates | tickets: Faber Peak Singapore, Harbour Front Centre, Harbour Front Tower 2, Sentosa Tour Desk | www.faberpeaksingapore.com | MRT CC 29, NE 1 Harbour Front*

2 RESORT WORLD SENTOSA ★
(138–139 C–D 3–4) *(P–Q6)*

The first things visitors see after they have crossed over the *Sentosa Gateway* bridge are the small towers and battlements of the *Universal Studios Singapore*, *(usually daily 10am–7pm | day pass adults 74, child ren 54 S$)*, part of the large Resort World Sentosa (RWS). The attractions in the gigantic amusement park have their roots in famous films; wherever you go, you will meet Shrek, the animal heroes from Madagascar and the dinosaurs from Jurassic Park. The developers even made a copy of Hollywood complete with a Walk of Fame *(Universal Studios usually* *daily 10am–7pm | 68–74 S$, prices and opening hours change according to the season)*. Dozens of restaurants, the wildest rollercoaster in South-East Asia and a live show with stuntmen and women from California will keep children and their parents entertained for at least a day. If you are feeling lucky, the *RWS Complex* is the right place for you: Singapore's second casino is located in the basement as is a *Musical Theatre (tickets from www.sistic.com.sg)*. The *Marine Life Park* offers everything water lovers ever dreamed of: the world's largest *Aquarium S.E.A. (daily 10am–7pm | day pass adults 38, children 28 S$)* also houses the *Maritime Experiential Museum (Mon–Thu 10am–7pm, Fri–Sun 10am–9pm | admission 5 S$)*, which tells the story of maritime trade. An extra 2 S$ on the cost of your day pass opens the doors to the new *Madame Tussauds (Mon–Fri 10am–7.30pm, Sat/Sun 10am–9pm | admission adults 39, children 29 S$)* waxworks. A few yards on, you come to the *Adventure Cove Water Park (daily 10am–6pm | day pass adults 36, children 26 S$)*. Animal lovers will probably head directly for *Dolphin Island (daily 10am–6pm | adults from 68, children from 58 S$)*. If you'd prefer to stroll around at your leisure, send the children to the *Kids Club (daily 10am–10pm | 12 S$ per hour)*. At nightfall, two spectacular, free displays await you at the water's edge: the *Crane Dance (daily 9pm)* sees two huge cranes imitating the remarkable courtship dance of their feathered namesakes. The *Lake of Dreams (daily 9.30pm)* is a fire, water and light show. If you get hungry, the choice is yours: the RWS has restaurants in every price segment. If you can't get enough of the fun, book a hotel room directly on the RWS Complex – say, at the *Hard Rock Hotel (Expensive)* or at the *Michael (Expensive)*. *www.rwsentosa.com | MRT NE 1, CC 29 Harbour Front, continue with Sentosa Express SE 1 Waterfront.*

3 SOUTHERN RIDGES
(132–133 A–F 3–6) *(A–D 5–7))*

One of the loveliest hiking trails in Singapore *(p. 107)* covers a distance of

KEEP FIT!

Early birds will find a perfect place for their activities as soon as the sun rises in the old *Botanic Gardens* **(128 A–B 1–4)** ***(C–D1)***: tai-chi, sword and fan dancing and gymnastics. Most of the trainers will not object if you simply join in; in fact they are usually delighted at your interest. If you prefer to train alone, you can take one of the jogging trails. Well-trained cyclists peddle around the island along the so-called *Park Connector (Signpost: PCN Park Connector Network)* that links the green areas of the city. Those who do not feel quite so energetic can choose one of the individual sections such as the one along the ● East Coast starting at *East Coast Park* **(0)** ***(N–S3)*** *(www.nparks.gov.sg | www.lifestylerecreation.com.sg)* heading east. Be warned: at the weekend, it seems as though all of Singapore is here having a good time! You can hire bicycles and inline skates every day at the small booths or so-called PCN pit stops along the route.

9 km (5.5 mi) and passes over three hills. It is made unique by spectacular bridges such as the wooden INSIDER TIP *Henderson Waves* – the highest pedestrian bridge in Singapore – and elevated paths on stilts at the height of the treetops. The trail begins in Hort Park and ends at the Vivo City shopping centre where you can get your breath back after all your hard work and reward yourself with an ice cream and the view of the sea. *www.nparks.gov.sg | MRT CC 27 Labrador Park, then bus 100 to Hort Park*

4 BEACHES

(138–139 A–E 4–6) (*🕮 O–R 6–8*)

Admittedly, the water along the busiest shipping route in the world could be cleaner but the good 3 km (almost 2 mi) of white sandy beaches on Sentosa – Siloso, Palawan and Tanjong – still have a certain amount of charm. The beaches are connected with each other by the Beach Train. This is a great place to chill out when the daytime tropical heat fades away in the evening: the New Year's Eve *Rave Party* is famous. But the *Pizzeria Trapizza* also attracts families and the *Café del Mar* young lovers to the beach on normal evenings. Water sports fans who are a bit wary of the seawater here can use the *Wave House (daily 10.30am–10.30pm, Wed, Sat, Sun 9am–11pm | from 45 S$ | www.wavehouse sentosa.com)* at Siloso Beach for – challenging – surfing on artificial breakers. The southernmost point in Asia is on a small island just off Sentosa's main beach. From here, you have a view of Singapore's southern islands, such as Kusu Island and St John's Island, of which some can be reached from the Cruise Center with the ferries from *Singapore Island Cruise and Ferry Services (ticket 18 S$ | 31 Marina Coastal Drive | Marina South Pier | tel. 65 34 93 39 | www.islandcruise.com.sg | MRT NS 28 Marina South Pier)*.

Siloso Beach – green-belt recreation in the true sense: palm trees, white sand and the city as the backdrop

5 UNDERWATER WORLD (138 A–B3) (*O6*)

The Underwater World on Sentosa, with its *Dolphin Lagoon* at the western tip of the island, is devoted to life beneath the waves. You will be able to pat dolphins *(190 S$)*, dine with sharks *(130 S$)* and have a footbath in the fish pools of the Underwater World. *Daily 10am–7pm | admission adults 29.90, children 20.60 S$ for both | www.underwaterworld.com.sg | blue, red Sentosa bus to Siloso Point*

6 IMBIAH LOOKOUT AMUSEMENT DISTRICT (138 B3–4) (*P6*)

You can take part in activities ranging from simply athletic to genuinely breathtaking in the area around the highest point on Sentosa, Mount Imbiah. The *Megazip (39 S$)* sets out on its long journey through the air on a steel cable from the hill to an island off the coast. Other attractions in the *Megazip Adventure Park (Mon–Fri 2pm–7pm, Sat/Sun 11am–7pm)*: the *Climbmax* mountain-climbing school *(39 S$)* and *Parajump (12 S$)*, with simulated parachute jumps from a height of a good 15 m (50 ft). A little further to the east, you can race down hill on a sledge in the *Skyline Luge Sentosa (daily 10am–9.30pm| from 15 S$)*.

7 VIVO CITY (138 C2) (*Q5*)

The shopping centre with a view of the harbour designed by the Japanese architect Toyo Ito reminds one of a spaceship. The white building, without any corners or sharp edges, houses branches of many of the top chains from Gap to Zara. Singapore's newest shopping paradise is made complete by a number of good restaurants with views of departing and arriving ships. This is also where you will find the city's most modern cinema with reclining seats; food is even served to guests in the auditorium of the ● *Golden Village*. There is a gigantic pool on the roof. *Daily 10am–10pm | 1 Harbourfront Walk/Sentosa Gateway | www.vivocity.com.sg | MRT NE 1 CC 29 HarbourFront*

IN OTHER DISTRICTS

BOTANIC GARDENS (128 A2–4) (*A1*)

Singapore's old Botanic Gardens are a tropical gem only a few minutes' walk away from the Orchard Road shopping street. In July 2015 they were named Singapore's first Unesco World Heritage Site. More than 2000 different plant species grow in the gigantic 128-acre grounds. There is a ● primary rainforest as well as manicured lawns, waterfalls, lakes, fern and rose gardens. The ● orchid garden, with species blooming all year round and more than 60,000 individual plants, is famous throughout the world. New sections show cacti, herbs, medicinal and water plants. There is a large playground for the children and they will also be fascinated by *Eco Garden* the copy of a primeval landscape. The attractions are made complete with restaurants and educational buildings.

Originally, the Botanic Gardens – as well as the predecessor laid out by Sir Stamford Raffles – were an experimental site for the commercial use of plants. Raffles concentrated on edible plants and spices and the botanist Henry Ridley started trial plantings of rubber trees, whose seed had been brought to Singapore from Brazil, in the middle of the 19th century. He was initially made fun of as 'Mad Riley' but he actually laid the foundations for the production of natural rubber that became one of the most important sectors of the South-East Asian economy. *Daily 5am–midnight | free admission | Orchid Garden daily 8.30am–7pm | admission 5 S$ | Jacob Ballas Children's Garden Tue–Sun 8am–7pm | free admission | 1 Cluny Road | entrance, corner of Holland Road | www.sbg.org.sg | MRT CC 19 Botanic Gardens | MRT NS 22 Orchard, then bus 7, 77, 106, 123, 174 ab Orchard Boulevard*

GEYLANG SERAI (O) *(🕮 d3)*

Malays settled here long before the arrival of the English and Chinese. Malay fishermen moved themselves here in 1840, after they were driven away from their stilt villages on the Singapore River by the English. Some of their descendants still moor their boats at East Coast Park. They take tourists out fishing with them for a small fee. Malay culture still characterises life in Geylang, especially on religious holidays, and the shops sell Malay products, such as at the *Joo Chiat Complex (1 Joo Chiat Road)* or the covered market, *Malay Village (daily 10am–10pm | 31 Geylang Serai)*. Wealthy Arabs and Malays had their magnificent villas – many of them built in a gingerbread-house style – erected in this part of the city. Geylang Serai is always splendidly decorated for Muslim holidays such as Hari Raya Puasa, the festive meal that marks the end of Ramadan fasting. *MRT CC9, EW 8 Paya Lebar*

HOLLAND VILLAGE (O) *(🕮 A1)*

Today's counterparts of Singapore's early settlers, the envoys of the banks and multinational companies, like to have their homes near Holland Village. Here, they are close to the city centre but still in a green environment. There are some inexpensive shops that cater to Western tastes in this district – especially in the *Holland Village Shopping Centre*, although it is not particularly attractive from the outside. The Indian newsagents on the street corners have a wide selection of international newspapers. There are many good restaurants – some of them serving Western food – especially on *Jalan Merah Saga*. If you feel like it, you will be able to find out a lot about the real life of the city and make contacts easily in the bars in Holland Village. On the left of Holland Avenue, a few free spirits have populated the old military housing area. On the right, a completely new, large shopping complex is due to open by 2017. *MRT CC 21 Holland Village | bus 7, 77, 106 from MRT NS 22 Orchard/Orchard Boulevard.*

TANGLIN VILLAGE (DEMPSEY HILL) (128 A–B 4–5) *(🕮 C–D2)*

Another one of Singapore's attractions lies hidden behind tall tropical trees between Holland Village and the inner city. Although the extensive area of Tanglin Village might not look particularly exciting at first glance, Singapore's Development Agency has declared the former military complex on the hill to be one of its priority projects. In 1860, the military forces built their barracks on what was once a nutmeg plantation just outside the gates of the then town. New life has since moved in with restaurants, wine shops, antique dealers and boutiques. It will take you a while if you intend to walk up the hill, but you will be rewarded with many interesting discoveries. These include fashionable meeting places like the *PS. Café*, as well as dealers in old Buddha statues such as *Shang Antique.* The number of Ferraris, Maseratis and Porsches parked here will make it clear that Dempsey Hill is the absolute hotspot for Singapore's smart set. The feeling of space, the old *black-and-white houses* and the tropical trees are what combine to make this district so attractive. *Diagonally opposite the Botanic Gardens | MRT NS 22 Orchard/Orchard Boulevard | then bus 7, 77, 106, 123, 174*

FURTHER AFIELD

EAST COAST PARK (O) *(N–S3)*
This park, which runs for miles along the east coast of the city state, is one of the Singaporeans' most popular excursion locations. That is why you should avoid visiting it at the weekend!
As the mood takes you, you can relax on the beach, hire a bicycle or inline skates, pitch your tent, go wakeboarding, barbecue or just go for a stroll along the seashore. A stop in one of the many seafood restaurants is especially recommendable. *bus 16 to Marine Terrace, then further through a underpass under the ECP Highway; bus 36 from Orchard Road or MRT CC 9/EW 8 Paya Lebar, then bus 76*

Green, tropical, luxuriant and full of pleasant surprises: Botanic Gardens

JURONG BIRD PARK (O) *(📖 b4)*
The largest bird park in South-East Asia is home to 9000 specimens of more than 600 species from all over the world including the largest collection of South-East Asian hornbills and South-American toucans, as well as the second-largest penguin show on earth. A single-gauge railway runs through the park. The largest aviary covers an area of five acres with a tropical forest, waterfall, artificial rain showers and rumbles of thunder that make the colourful tropical birds seek cover. In the *Pools Amphitheater* there's a *Highflyers Show* several times a day in which trained birds perform amazing artistic feats. *Daily 8.30am–6pm | admission adults 28, children 18 S$ | lunch with the parrots noon–2pm, adults 22, children 17 S$ | tel. 63 60 85 60 | combined ticket available, for Zoo, night safari and river safari | 2 Jurong Hill | tel. 62 65 00 22 | www.birdpark.com.sg | MRT EW 27 Boon Lay, continue with bus 194 or 251*

Feathered diversity: Jurong Bird Park

LIAN SHAN HUANG LIN MONASTERY (O) *(📖 d4)*
This monastery complex from the year 1908 is now a national monument. This is because it not only includes the temples in memory of the birth and death of Buddha but also the neighbouring Taoist Cheng Hunag Miao Temple dedicated to the city's god. The Buddhist monastery is dominated by the pagoda whose bells chime in the wind. Three courtyards lead into the individual temple halls where magnificently carved statues of Buddha await the visitors. *184 Jalan Toa Payoh | www.shuanglin.org | MRT NS 19 Toa Payoh*

INSIDER TIP MEMORIES AT OLD FORD FACTORY (O) *(📖 b4)*
In 1941, the Ford factory in Singapore became the first plant in South-East Asia to produce automobiles. The city has converted the historical buildings into a fascinating memorial site to Singapore's experiences during the Japanese occupation (1942–45). The Japanese renamed the city Syonan-To, 'Light of the South'. But they ruled with such brutality that the Singaporeans have not been able to forget their atrocities to this day. *Mon–Sat 9am–5.30pm, Sun noon–5.30 pm | admission 3 S$ | 351 Upper Bukit Timah Road | www.nas.gov.sg/moff | MRT NS 2 Bukit Batok, then bus 173; MRT CC 14 Botanic Gardens, then bus 170/171*

SINGAPORE ZOOLOGICAL GARDENS, NIGHT SAFARI & RIVER SAFARI ★ (O) *(📖 c3)*
The beautiful Singapore Zoo was conceived as an 'open zoo' in 1973 – which means that most of the animals are kept

in large open enclosures. Wherever possible, bars were done away with and deep trenches filled with water separate the visitors from those being visited. The *Night Safari* is a real highlight that no visitor to Singapore should miss. Both the Zoo and Night Safari have received many awards. The *Conservation Centre* provides full information on the institution's activities. You can see the 3600 animals being fed at various times between 9am and 5pm – If you wish you can register for the *Jungle Breakfast (daily 9am–10.30am | admission adults 33, children 23 S$ | book via tel. 63 60 85 60 or saleshotline.wrs@wrs.com.sg)* with the orang-utans.

The *River Safari* is a further highlight – a 20-ha, 100m-S$ tropical jungle you can explore by boat. The journey takes you through 10 global ecosystems such as the Nile Delta, along the Mississippi or up the Amazon. Children love to see the pandas Kai Kai and Jia Jia in their Panda Forest enclosure on the river. There are also the smaller red pandas.

The *Night Safari (daily 7.30pm–midnight, tickets on sale until 11pm | admission adults 42, children 28 S$)* opens 90 minutes after the zoo closes: the 40-ha (98 ac) site is one and a half times the size of the daytime zoo. Torches blaze at the entrance, and the site is bathed in a dim glow; special lamps illuminate the 1000 animals (110 different species) until midnight. Apply insect repellent generously! At the entrance there is a small map suggesting various signposted routes. When you get tired, let the railway carry you around. Be sure to leave enough time to get here; the journey from the city takes a good 1¼ hours. *Daily 8.30am–6pm | admission adults 32, children 23 S$; people celebrating their birthday get in free (bring your passport!); Park Hopper combined tickets for Zoo, Night Safari, River Safari and Jurong Bird Park are better value | 80 Mandai Lake Road | tel. 62 69 34 11 | www.wrs.com.sg | www.zoo.com.sg | bus 171 Mandai Lake Road, then cross the road and continue with bus 138 to the terminus; MRT NS 16 Ang Mo Kio, continue with bus 138; MRT NS 4 Choa Chu Kang, then continue with bus 927 | The Singapore Attractions Express collects you from some hotels and underground stations (www.saex.com.sg)*

FOCUS ON SPORT

The annual night-time Formula 1 race sends scenes of the city into the living rooms of billions of people around the world.

If you are interested in sport in Singapore, you will find all you need to know on the *Singapore Sports Council (www.ssc.gov.sg)* website. Singapore's pride and joy is the *Singapore Sports Hub* **(O)** ***(N2)****(www.sportshub.com.sg)*, the national stadium which hosts major sporting events. The roof can be opened, the seats are cooled and there's room for 55,000 spectators.

The Padang is the main sports arena in the city centre. *Singapore Cricket Club (www.scc.org.sg)* still plays on its old ground and this is also where rugby teams fight it out *(www.scrugbyseens.com)*. Water-sports fans can watch sailing regattas in the windy winter months and dragon-boat races *(www.sdba.org.sg)* and surfing *(www.wakeboard.com)* all year round.

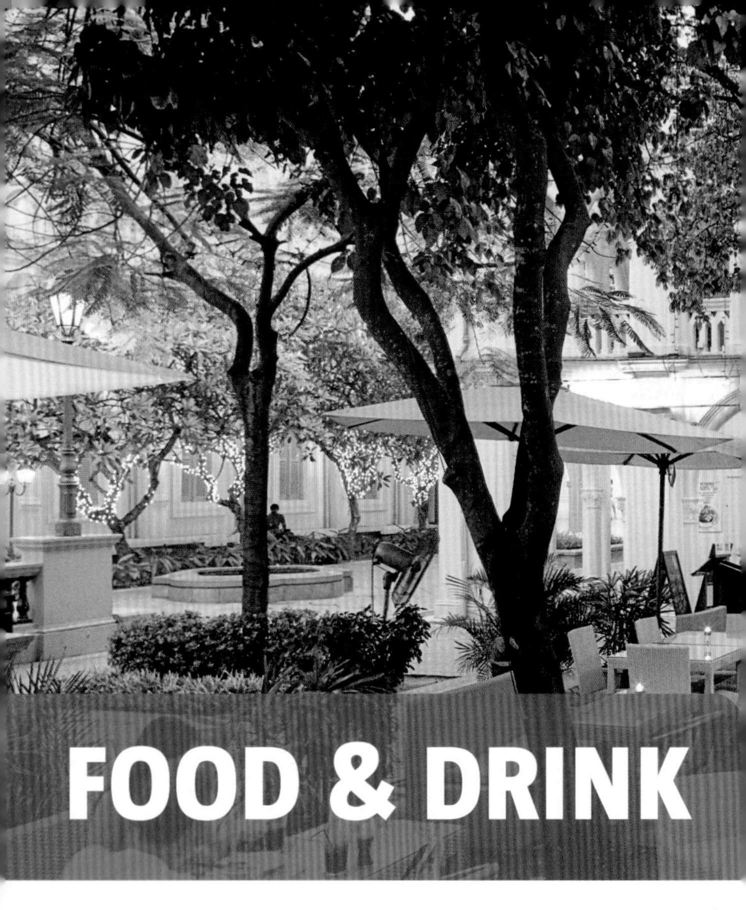

FOOD & DRINK

High-quality food is something Singaporeans take very seriously: they talk a lot about eating, and good chefs are held in high esteem. The city state offers enormous variety in a very small area. You will not only be able to savour all of Asia's cuisines here but the very best of Australia and Europe as well.

The servings are often smaller than at home – this applies especially to street booths. Eat the way the locals do and do not gorge yourself; the rule is: INSIDER TIP it is better to eat less but do it more often. That will also make it easier for you to try out all the different national styles of cooking.

The best way to do that is in one of the so-called hawker centres a collection of small cookshops. They used to be outside in the open air but today they can be found in the basement or upper floors of all the large shopping centres and at regular food markets. You sit down on plastic chairs to eat after you have chosen a dish directly from one of the pans; drinks are sold at an extra booth.

In addition to Chinese, Indian and Malay cooking, Singapore has its own unique style: *Peranakan* cuisine that developed along the Straits of Malacca. The Peranakan culture was established by the early immigrants and combines Chinese with

The magic word is: variety. Singapore is a melting pot for all the cuisines of our world – from China to Italy and Malaysia to France

Malay and European influences. In Singapore, you can dine for 4 S$ or 400 S$. Seven percent value-added tax (GST) and a service charge of 10 percent are added to the prices on the menu. Nobody expects to be tipped. Restaurants can become very expensive if you order alcohol. There are extremely high taxes on alcoholic beverages and a beer can easily cost 7.50 S$.

CAFÉS & TEA HOUSES

INSIDER TIP **40 HANDS** (134 C4) (*⑪ F5*)

This retro café in a shophouse from the 1930s, in the heart of the fashionable Tiong Bahr district, serves one of the best cups of coffee in town. There are also sandwiches and hotdogs at lunchtime. *Closed Mon | 78 Yong Siak Street | #01–12 | MRT EW 17 Tiong Bahru*

TWG, the oasis in the middle of the hustle and bustle of shopping in the mall

CEDELE (129 D4) *(F2)*
Chain of cafés in many shopping districts; the most popular place for Western women in Singapore. Cedele serves organic cakes and fair-trade coffee. E.g.: *Daily 10am–10pm | Wheelock Place | 501 Orchard Road | #03–14 | www.cededepot.com | MRT NS 22 Orchard*

JEWEL CAFÉ & BAR (131 D2) *(0)*
They roast the beans on the premises of this coffee paradise in Little India; it's well worth taking a look at the place. *Sun–Thu 9am–10pm Fri/Sat 9am–11pm | 129 Rangoon Road | MRT NE 8 Farrer Park*

KITH (139 F5) *(S7)*
Australian café with a huge menu on one of Singapore's prettiest spots: bang in the centre of the new restaurant area at the marina on Sentosa. On the right, a Greek and a pizzeria, on the left, bars and a Belgian – but Kith is one of a kind: the food is fresh, plentiful and lovingly prepared. The cocktails and smoothies help you keep a cool head while dreaming of that million-dollar yacht! *Wed–Mon 8am–10pm | 31 Ocean Way | Sentosa Cove | www.kith.com.sg | MRT NE 1 Harbour Front, then bus 188 R and on foot*

PS. CAFE AT HARDING
(128 A4) *(C2)*
Artists and writers congregate here under the tropical trees to enjoy brunch or afternoon tea, the Australian-style food and the gigantic chocolate cakes. *Mon–Thu 11.30am–midnight, Fri/Sat 9.30am–2am, Sun 9.30am–midnight | 28b Harding Road, Tanglin Village | tel. 64 79 33 43 | MRT NS 22 Orchard, then bus 7, 77, 106, 123, 174 from Orchard Boulevard*

INSIDER TIP TEA CHAPTER
(135 F4) *(H6)*
Probably the most famous tea house in Chinatown. You can experience a tea

ceremony too and buy the choice leaves. *Daily 11am–11pm | 9 and 11 Neil Road | www.tea-chapter.com.sg | tel. 62 26 11 75 | MRT NE 4 Chinatown*

TOAST BOX (129 F4–5) (🗺 G2)
Here you'll get only classic food – but that's a bit of an understatement: the classic breakfast of kopi (coffee) or teh (tea) and kaya toast (with coconut and egg jam). Watching the typical Singaporean way of preparing the coffee is a feast for the eyes in itself. *In many large shopping centres, e.g. daily 7.30am–10pm | The Paragon | #02–08a | www.toastbox.com.sg | MRT NS 22 Orchard*

TWG ★ (129 E4) (🗺 F2)
The charm of good old Europe in the heart of Singapore's most modern shopping centres: the TWG tea house has developed into a popular meeting place. In the meantime, there are several branches in the Marina Bay Sands complex. Not without reason: in their colourful large tea tins, the young entrepreneurs sell many of their own unique blends. *Daily 10am–10pm | ION | 2 Orchard Turn | #02-21 | www.twgtea.com | MRT NS 22 Orchard*

HAWKER CENTRES & FOOD COURTS

Most of the snack centres with their many small booths open early in the morning for breakfast and work until late at night. The most stylish hawker centre is the ★ *Lau Pa Sat Festival Market* (136 B4) (🗺 J5–6) *(MRT DT 17 Downtown)* on Robinson Road. There was already a market here in 1822. As part of the redevelopment of Chinatown, the Singapore Tourism Board revamped *Smith Street* (135 F4) (🗺 H5) *(MRT NE 4 Chinatown)* and turned it into a strip of restaurants *(MRT NE 4 Chinatown)*.
The finest *food court* is on the roof of the *Vivo City* (138 C2) (🗺 D8) shopping centre, directly by the sea: the INSIDER TIP *Food Republic@Vivo City (# 3 | 1 Harbour Front Walk | MRT NE 1 Harbourfront)* is laid

MARCO POLO HIGHLIGHTS

★ TWG
Favourite meeting place for tea in the best shopping centre in town → p. 65

★ Lau Pa Sat Festival Market
Hawker food in a fairytale hall – go at lunchtime when the food is really fresh → p. 65

★ The Clifford Pier
An air of the glorious days of ocean liners with fine Asian specialities thrown in → p. 67

★ The Knolls
Enjoy the sunset on a terrace designed by Norman Foster → p. 67

★ Supertree by Indochine
Dine on an artificial tree high above the new Botanic Gardens → p. 68

★ Din Tai Fung
Watch as they make the dim sums, which then taste delicious too → p. 68

★ The Intan
Delve into Singapore's Peranakan eating culture → p. 69

★ The Song of India
Excellent Indian cooking – served with charm in a historical colonial house → p. 69

out like an old Chinese village. The *Maxwell Road Food Centre* (135 F4) (*H6*) *(MRT DT 19, NE 4 Chinatown)* in Chinatown ressembles an open market. You'll also find some very good *hawker centres* alongside the Esplanade Culture Centre in *Makan-sutra Gluttons Bay*. In the basement (B4) of the *ION Orchard* centre, every day at 11am, you can follow the INSIDER TIP *Local Food Trail (tel. 62 38 82 28)* to get to know the local specialities.

GOURMET RESTAURANTS

André (135 E4–5) *(G6)*
The man who cooks here is a real artist: Chef André Chiang's philosophy is to create meals using the freshest products on the market. The eight-course tasting menu is oriented on concepts such as 'pure' or 'artisan'. There is a new menu every day. Located in an old shophouse in Chinatown. *Wed–Fri noon–2pm and Tue–Sun 7pm–11pm | 41 Bukit Pasoh Road | tel. 65 34 88 80 | www.restaurantandre.com | MRT EW 16, NE 3 Outram Park*

Iggy's (129 D4) *(E–F2)*
The tiny restaurant with the strong Japanese influence in the kitchen is one of the city's best. The open kitchen is larger than the dining room which seats only 40 guests. Reservation essential! *Mon, Thu–Sat noon–1.30pm and Mon–Sat 7pm–9.30pm | The Hilton Hotel | 581 Orchard Road | #3 | tel. 67 32 22 34 | www.iggys.com.sg | MRT NS 22 Orchard*

Raffles Hotel (136 C1) *(K3)*
Not only business executives appreciate the restaurant in the rustic Long Bar Steak House. The Sunday brunch in the Billiard Room, with its abundance of delicious food, has become legendary. *1 Beach Road | tel. 64 31 61 56 | www.raffles.com/singapore | MRT NS 25, EW 13 City Hall*

Jaan (136 B1) *(J3)*
One of the 50 best restaurants in Asia, with a spectacular view from the 70th floor. Head chef Julien Royer offers sublime fusion cuisine. *Mon–Sat noon–2.30pm and 7pm–10pm | Equinox Complex Swissôtel The Stamford | #70 | 2 Stamford Road | tel. 68 37 33 22 | www.jaan.com.sg | MRT NS 25, EW 13 Cityhall*

Punjab Grill (137 D–E 3–4) *(K–L5)*
Although the name might not lead you to expect very much, master chef Jiggs Kalra's cooking will carry you back to the India of old. He has modernised the cuisine of North India with great finesse. *Daily 11.30am–3.30pm and 6.30–11pm | Marina Bay Sands | #B1–01a, Galeria Level | tel. 66 88 73 95 | www.punjabgrill.com.sg | MRT CE 1, DT 16 Bay Front*

Tóng Lè Private Dining (136 C3–4) *(J5)*
Many consider this to be the best Chinese gourmet restaurant in Singapore at the moment. Alongside exquisite food served in an intimate atmosphere, there's also a fantastic view of the sea. Reservations only. *Mon–Sat 11.30am–3pm, 6pm–11pm | OUE Tower 08 and 10 | 60 Coll-yer Quay | tel. 66 34 32 33 | www.tong-le.com.sg | MRT EW 14, NS 26 Raffles Place*

The classy surroundings at The Knolls make it hard to focus on the fabulous food

RESTAURANTS: EXPENSIVE

THE BLACK SWAN (136 B4) *(🗺 J5)*
Western luxury behind a Singaporean art-deco façade. Bankers meet here for lunch, chic couples for dinner over champagne. *Mon–Fri 11.30am–2.30pm, tea 2pm–5pm, Mon–Sat 5pm–10.30pm | 19 Cecil Street | tel. 81813305 | www.theblackswan.com.sg | MRT EW 14, NS 26 Raffles Place*

THE CLIFFORD PIER ★
(136 C3) *(🗺 J–K5)*
The tasteful surroundings at this spacious restaurant in the former arrivals hall for overseas liners remind you of the 1920s – thanks, too, to the musical accompaniment until late in the evening. On the plates you'll find refined Asian street food and a few classic Western dishes. Head chef Ken Zheng has given a few of his father's recipes a new lease of life. The mix on the menu is reminiscent of Singapore's own colourful ethnic composition. *Daily noon–2.30pm, tea 3.30pm–5.30pm, dinner 6.30pm–10pm, late supper Sun–Thu 10pm–midnight, Fri/Sat 10pm–1am | 80 Collyer Quay | Clifford Pier | tel. 65975266 | www.fullertonbayhotel.com | MRT EW 14, NS 26 Raffles Place*

THE KNOLLS ★
(138–139 C–D5) *(🗺 Q7)*
It is difficult to imagine a more beautiful view – and it would be equally difficult to beat the food. You can have your meal sitting on the sea-view terrace of this colonial house on Sentosa, which was restored by leading architect Norman Foster. After dinner, the ● INSIDER TIP lounge on the first floor is the ideal place to relax with a drink by candlelight. The cuisine is modern Asian. *Daily 7am–11pm | in the Capella Hotel on Sentosa | tel. 65134275 | www.capellasingapore.com | from Vivo City (MRT CC 29, NE 1 HarbourFront) with the Sentosa Express (S2 Imbiah) or by bus; also pick-up service*

INSIDER TIP PRIMA TOWER REVOLVING RESTAURANTR
(139 D2) *(🗺 Q5)*
Diners in this revolving restaurant can enjoy a view over the harbour and exquisite cooking. The decoration is from the 1960s; the Peking duck is famous. Come at lunchtime – because of the lower prices. *Mon–Sat 11am–2.30pm, Sun 10.30am–2.30pm,*

daily 6.30pm–10.30pm | 201 Keppel Road | tel. 62 72 88 22 | www.pfs.com.sg | MRT NE 1 Harbourfront, then bus 10, 100 towards city centre

Fusion specialist above the rooftops of Singapore: Justin Quek from Sky on 57

SKY ON 57 (137 D3–4) (*K–L5*)
Chef Justin Quek offers French/Asian cuisine for gourmets. The breathtaking view from the *Skypark* of the *Marina Bay Sands* down onto the city and the sea is thrown in for free. The *bar (daily 11am–11.45pm)* is a gem in its own right. *Mon–Fri 7am–10.30am, Sat/Sun 7am–11am, daily noon–5pm and 6pm–10.30pm | Sands Sky Park Tower 1 | #57 | in the Marina Bay Sands complex | tel. 66 88 88 57 | www.marinabaysands.com/restaurants/sky-on-57.html | MRT CE 1, DT 16 Bay Front*

SUPERTREE BY INDOCHINE ★ (137 E4) (*L5*)
A one-of-a-kind location: the Supertree is only at the *Gardens by the Bay*. The restaurant and rooftop bar are situated on two levels in the metal tropical trees, high above the gardens. Owner Michael Ma, a Lao who made his fortune in Singapore, serves fusion cuisine with Laotian, Cambodian and Vietnemese-French influences. *Sun–Thu noon– 1pm, Fri/Sat noon–2am | 18 Marina Gardens Drive | #03–01 | Gardens by the Bay | tel. 66 94 84 89 | indochine-group.com/home/locsingapore-supertree.php | MRT CE 1, DT 16 Bayfront*

THE TIPPLING CLUB (136 A5) (*H6*)
Do you want to have your steak melted and your fish as a drink? If you do, the Tippling Club is the place for you – this is where Ryan Clift prepares molecular food. Some people come just to enjoy the INSIDER TIP cocktails. *Mon–Fri noon–3pm, Mon–Sat 6pm–open end | 38 Tanjong Pagar Road | tel. 64 75 22 17 | www.tipplingclub.com | MRT EW 15 Tanjong Pagar*

RESTAURANTS: MODERATE

DIN TAI FUNG ★ 141 D3–4) (*K–L5*)
Dim Sum live: here you can watch the chefs at work while you're queuing for a table. It's worth the wait: the mini dumplings are a dream, and the service is hard to beat, too. *In many shopping centres, e. g. Sun–Thu 10.30am–10.30pm, Fri/Sat 10am–11.30pm | Marina Bay Sands | 2 Bayfront Av. | #B2–63 | tel. 66 34 99 69 | www.dintaifung.com.sg | MRT CE 1, DT 16 Bayfront*

INSIDER TIP **EAST COAST SEAFOOD CENTRE** (0) (*d4*)
This is the perfect place to try Singapore's national disht *Black Pepper Crab*. The

entire row of restaurants along the coast specialises in seafood. The view of the ocean is romantic but the restaurants themselves provide a rather sober Chinese atmosphere with plastic stools and neon lighting. 1206 *Upper East Coast Road | preferably by Taxi*

THE INTAN ★ (0) (*d4*)
Here you will be able to delve deep into Peranakan culture: first of all you are shown the authentic house and then served a home-made Peranakan dish for lunch, at tea-time or for dinner. Only by appointment. *69 Joo Chiat | tel. 64 40 11 48 | MRT EW 7 Eunos, then bus 7, 24, 67*

INSIDER TIP **NANBANTEI** (129 E4) (*F1*)
Nobody would expect there to be a good place to eat in this shopping centre, but the Japanese restaurant has its regular clients: the fresh salmon rolled in bacon and the raw mackerel are absolutely delicious. But this is a very down-to-earth place, best enjoyed sitting at the counter directly in front of the charcoal grill. *Daily noon–2.30pm, 6–10.30pm | 14 Scotts Road | Far East Plaza | #05–132 | tel. 67 33 56 66 | www.nanbantei.com.sg | MRT NS 22 Orchard*

THE SONG OF INDIA ★
(129 E3) (*F1*)
One of the most exquisite Indian restaurants in the city. You will be delighted by the charm of the old colonial house although you might find the interior decoration a bit kitschy. But you will not be able to fault chef Millind Sovani's excellent cooking. *Daily noon–3pm, 6–11pm | 33 Scotts Road | tel. 68 36 00 55 | www.thesongofindia.com | MRT NS 22 Orchard*

SPRING COURT (135 F3) (*H5*)
Singapore's oldest family-run restaurant serves traditional Chinese cooking at reasonable prices. The locals love to eat the fish dishes. *Daily 11am–2.30pm, 6pm–10.30pm | 52–56 Upper Cross Street | tel. 64 49 50 30 | www.springcourt.com.sg | MRT NE 4, DT 19 Chinatown*

TRUE BLUE (136 B1) (*J3*)
Chef Baba Ben, as the Singaporeans call Benjamin Seck, cooks in the traditional Peranakan style – a mixture of Chinese, Malay and European cuisines. The recipes still come from his mother Nyonya Daisy Seah. The restaurant is located next to the Peranakan Museum. *Daily 11am–2.30pm, 6–9.30pm | 47/49 Armenian Street | tel. 64 40 04 49 | www.truebluecuisine.com | MRT CC 2 Bras Basah | MRT EW 13, NS 25 Cityhall, then bus 197*

THE WHITE RABBIT
(128 A4) (*C2*)
Chef Daniel Sia serves modern European food with a strong touch of Britain in the former garrison chapel. Many guests come simply because the cocktails are so good. *Tue–Fri noon–2.30pm, 6.30–10.30pm, Sat/Sun 10.30am–2.30pm, 6.30–10.30pm | 39c Harding Road | tel. 64 73 99 65 | www.thewhiterabbit.com.sg | MRT NS 22 Orchard, then bus 7, 77, 106, 123 from Orchard Boulevard*

RESTAURANTS: BUDGET

INSIDER TIP **328 KATONG LAKSA**
(138 A6) (*S2*)
You will not come across any tourists in this eatery. The street restaurant is in the heart of Katong, the old Peranakan district. 328 Katong Laksa won the 'Laksa War' against the neighbouring restaurants and Singaporeans come from the other side of town to enjoy the tasty soup that only costs 4 S$ here. *Daily 8am–10pm | 51–53 East Coast Road/Ceylon Road | bus 14 from Orchard Road*

LOCAL SPECIALITIES

Bah Kut Teh – spicy herb soup with pork and offal
Bak Kwa – Shreded pork, brushed with honey, then grilled: doesn't look very appetising, but tastes delicious
Chai Tow Kway/Carrot Cake – a kind of pancake with spring onions and sweet black sauce; not at all like the usual carrot cake
Char Kway Teow – fried, flat noodles with sweet, black sauce from the wok, with small Chinese sausages, soy sprouts, eggs and garlic
Chicken Rice – gently cooked chicken with various sauces: pure poetry! Originally from the Chinese province of Hainan, it is now Singapore's national dish
Dim Sum – dumplings with meat, shrimp or vegetable filling, steamed in typical small baskets
Hokkien Mee – yellow noodles fried in a wok: with pork or squid and vegetables
Kaya Toast – sweet breakfast pudding made with milk, eggs and coconut milk on toast
Laksa – the noodles in the famous spicy soup are thick and yellow; served with pieces of chicken or fish, tofu cubes and coconut milk or tamarind juice (photo left)
Nasi Lemak – classic Malay breakfast of sticky rice cooked in coconut milk and wrapped in a banana leaf; served with small sardines and plenty of chilli
Rojak – tropical salad of cucumber, pineapple, mango, grilled tofu, tamarind juice, pieces of fried noodles with shrimp paste and chopped peanuts
Roti Prata – a kind of Indian pancake made with thin batter and served with a variety of fillings – most of them vegetarian. Stuffed with lamb or chicken, the pancakes are known as Murtabak; usually comes with curry sauce
Satay – chunks of chicken, lamb, beef or squid are marinated in hot spices and then grilled over charcoal, traditionally served with peanut sauce, cucumber and raw red onion (photo right)

BROTZEIT ☼
(138 C2) (*⊡ D8*)
If you have had enough of chicken and rice, you might like to try the dripping and liver sausage sandwiches at Brotzeit in the Vivo City. They are reasonably priced and there is a free view of the water. *Mon–Thu noon–midnight,*

Fri/Sat noon–1.30am, Sun 11am–midnight | 1 Harbourfront Walk | Vivo City | #01–149–151 | tel. 62 72 88 15 | www.brotzeit.co | MRT NE 1, CC 29 Harbourfront | branches: in 313@Somerset (Orchard Road) and in the Raffles City shopping centre

INSIDER TIP **NEW EVEREST KITCHEN** (130 C3) (*J1*)
No-frills ambience but tasty Nepalese-Tibetan food: if you eat here, you feel like you are at the base of an 8000-m (26,000 ft)- high mountain. The *Momos* (dumplings stuffed with meat) are just as tasty as the *Ladyfingers* (fried okra). In the heart of Little India. *Wed–Mon 11am–3pm, 5pm–11pm | 518 Macpherson | tel. 68 44 41 70 | www.neweverestkitchen.com*

KOMALA VILAS RESTAURANT (130 C4) (*J1*)
The most popular – and probably best – Indian vegetarian restaurant in the city. Here, you will be served all kinds of Indian bread, a great variety of rice dishes and lentils and spinach in many variations. *Daily 11am–3.30pm, 6pm–10.30pm | tel. 62 93 69 80 | www.komalavilas.com.sg | 76–78 Serangoon Road | MRT NE 7 Little India*

INSIDER TIP **OUR VILLAGE** (136 B3) (*J5*)
This restaurant on the fifth floor of a shophouse on Boat Quay scores with an unbeatable combination of good food and a fantastic panorama. You leave the hustle and bustle behind you as soon as you enter the welcoming rooftop terrace where you will be served dishes from North India and Sri Lanka. *Daily 6pm–11.30pm | minimum charge 35 S$ per person |46 Boat Quay | tel. 65 38 30 58 | MRT EW 14, NS 26 Raffles Place*

SINGAPORE ZAM ZAM (131 E5) (*K2*)
A well-established Arab restaurant opposite the Sultan Mosque: the world of the *Murtabak*, freshly baked, salty pancakes filled with minced lamb, onions or egg. *Daily 8am–11pm | 697 Northbridge Road | tel. 62 98 62 30 | MRT DT 14, EW 12 Bugis*

INSIDER TIP **TRAPIZZA** (138 B4) (*P6*)
The name is a mix of trapeze and pizza: Singapore's first trapeze school belongs to the restaurant. Both are run by the Hotel Shangri-La in the middle of the sandy beach on Sentosa Island. The unassuming pizzeria's tables and chairs are placed on the sand, the food is delicious, and your gaze will sweep over the sea with the ships that appear to be close enough to reach out and touch bobbing up and down on it. *Daily 11.30am–9.30pm | 101 Siloso Road | Sentosa | tel. 63 76 26 62 | MRT NE1 HarbourFront, then the bus (blue/red/green line) to the terminus at Siloso Beach*

LOW BUDGET

Visit one of the countless *hawker centres* at intersections and in the basement of almost all shopping centres. You will be able to savour all of the delicacies Asia has to offer at prices starting at 4 S$. You needn't worry about the quality. The *hawkers* are closely inspected.

If you are thirsty, you can always ask for ice water. The refreshing drink is usually served free of charge to accompany your meal in the restaurants in the city – but many tourists forget to ask for it. In any case, it is perfectly safe to drink.

SHOPPING

> **WHERE TO START?**
> **Orchard Road (129 D–F 4–5, 134 A–B 5–6) (*🕮 E–H 1–3*):** Start your spree on one of the most beautiful shopping avenues in the world. The heat and heavy downpours, however, mean a lot of Singapore's shopping takes place in air-conditioned precincts. Start in the luxury shops in **ION Orchard**, move on, under or above ground, past hundreds of shops to the **Takashimaya** department store. Cross the street, ending up at **The Paragon** or **Tangs**.

Many people think that the ringing of the cash registers is actually the secret national anthem of the city state.

The most famous shopping boulevard in Singapore is ● *Orchard Road* (129 D–F 4–5, 130 A–B 5–6) (*🕮 E–H 1–3*). No matter what you are looking for, you can be almost sure of finding it here. There are several department stores and hundreds – if not thousands – of retail shops in this district alone; and the number is rising all the time. This applies to the entire inner-city area: even the *Esplanade* cultural centre has a whole row of small boutiques. *Marina Bay Sands* has become the top address for lovers of luxury art-

Spending money as the elixir of life: I spend, therefore I am – is the motto of the Singaporean's favourite leisure-time activity

icles; the architectural highlight *Vivo City* has shops with a sea view. You will discover international chains such as Body Shop, Uniqlo and Zara in most of the malls. The shops are open seven days a week, usually from 10am to 10pm. At times, such as during the Christmas and Chinese New Year's festivities, the shopping centres stay open until 11pm.
It is still possible to find bargains: depending on the exchange rate, ladies' shoes and clothing are often cheaper than in Europe; the same applies to electronic articles, cameras and CDs. Be careful about prices that appear to be below the dealer's cost price; there is usually a catch. The accessories for the supposedly super-cheap video camera are often missing or there is no international guarantee. Or, if somebody wants to bring goods that are not in

stock at the moment to your hotel, you will probably find yourself confronted with items that you had no intention of buying. Therefore: do not pay for anything until you receive the goods! You can bargain to your heart's content in small shops but, as a rule, the large department stores in the inner city have fixed prices. These are often 10–20 percent above those you could get elsewhere after long-drawn-out haggling.
In order to avoid irritation later, look for the 'case trust' and 'QJS' signs on the shops where you make your purchases; these are awarded by the consumer protection organisation and the Union of Jewellers as an assurance of quality. If you still have complaints, call the toll-free Tourist-Hotline *(Mon–Fri 9am–6pm | tel. 1800 736 20 00)*. A seven-percent Goods and Service Tax (GST) is added to most articles and services. Visitors can have the tax refunded if their purchases exceed 100 S$. In 2012 Singapore introduced electronic processing of *tax refunds*. In shops you receive not only a receipt but also a 'e-TRS Ticket' when you present your passport. Take this to the self-help kiosk at the airport or cruise ship terminal and have the amount of tax refunded to your credit card account. You'll find details at *www.iras.gov.sg.*

Where shopping is raised to an art form: colourful sculptures at the entrance to the ION centre

BOOKS

INSIDER TIP BOOKS ACTUALLY
(134 C4) *(F5)*
This literary book shop is favourite meeting place, too. Situated in one of Singapore's most attractive streets, you can lose track of time on a Saturday morning here or at the café next door. *Sun/Mon 10am–6pm, Tue–Sat 10am–8pm | 9 Yong Siak Street | www.booksactually.com | MRT EW 17 Tiong Bahru*

KINOKUNIYA ★ (129 E5) *(F–G2)*
This is considered the largest bookshop in South-East Asia and also has a stock of books and magazines from many foreign countries, as well as an exceptionally good

selection of Asian literature in English. *391 Orchard Road | #04–20B/C | Ngee Ann City | MRT NS 22 Orchard*

TIMES (129 F5) (G2)
Local book store chain with English-language literature, loads of magazines and stationery. Many outlets, e. g. Times Bookstores at Centrepoint. *176 Orchard Road | Centrepoint | #04–08/09/10/11 | www.timesbookstores.com.sg | MRT NS 23 Somerset*

LADIES' SHOES

Ladies' shoes are one of the many bargain products you will find in Singapore. The latest models are frequently half the price that they cost in Europe. However, they are usually only available in sizes up to 6½ (US. 9). The shoe departments of the following stores offer the widest selection: *Metro* (129 F4–5) (G2) *(290 Orchard Road | in Paragon)*, *Tangs Orchard* (129 E4) (F2) *(310 Orchard Road)* and *Takashimaya* (129 E5) (F2) *(391 Orchard Road | Ngee Ann City). All: MRT NS 22 Orchard*

SHOPPING CENTRES

313@SOMERSET ★ (129 F5) (G2)
This department store has become the Singaporeans' favourite: it has four halls with the best shops in the city. And there is much more: the *Food Republic food court* on the fifth floor is like a trip to all the countries in Asia, the *Brotzeit* and *Marché* restaurants also cater to European tastes. *313 Orchard Road | www.313somerset.com.sg | MRT NS 23 Somerset*

THE CATHAY
(130 B5–6) (H–J3)
Singapore's young crowd flock to The Cathay. The new mall behind the Art Deco facade of a 1935 cinema has amusement arcades and cinemas under the roof and boutiques on the lower floors. *2 Handy Road | MRT CC 1 NS 24 NE 6 Dhoby Ghaut*

ION ORCHARD ★
(129 E4) (F2)
The Orchard has luxury goods from all around the world. You will be able to spend days in the main attraction on Orchard Road. There are restaurants, a food court in the basement and a post office. The design is ultra-modern. You are sure to lose your way – and that is just what the shop owners want. *2 Orchard Turn | www.ionorchard.com | MRT NS 22 Orchard*

MARCO POLO HIGHLIGHTS

★ Kinokuniya
For bookworms – not only when it's wet outside → p. 74

★ 313@Somerset
The Singaporeans' favourite address → p. 75

★ ION Orchard
Singapore's exclusive mall with more than 300 shops → p. 75

★ Marina Bay Sands
The newest and most luxurious shopping centre: you can easily spend a full day here → p. 76

★ Tanglin Village (Dempsey Hill)
Today the in-crowd meets where soldiers used to drill → p. 80

★ Mustafa
Everything you ever wanted to buy – around the clock → p. 80

Saving energy: at the MBS rink your skates glide over plastic, not ice

MARINA BAY SANDS ★
(137 D3–4) (*🗺 K–L5*)
Here, you will find all of the world's top luxury brands under a single (large) roof. There is even a copy of a section of Venice: almost-authentic gondolieri will punt you along a canal running through the middle of the building. The store's own skating rink only appears to cool you down: its surface is made of plastic instead of ice. Louis Vuitton's spectacular shop has opened its doors on an island in Marina Bay. There is no lack of top-class restaurants and there are less expensive chain shops and restaurants in the rear section of the mall. *www.marinabaysands.com | MRT CE 1, DT 16 Bayfront*

NGEE ANN CITY (129 E5) (*🗺 F–G2*)
The Japanese department store chain *Takashimaya* has taken over one wing of this temple to consumerism. The top floors are reserved for the exclusive boutiques of Armani and Co.; young, off-the-peg fashion has found its place on the basement floors. Other attractions here include: good restaurants, hairdressers, the gigantic Kinokuniya bookshop and galleries. On Chinese holidays, many stands with ● local delicacies are set up in the basement and you can often taste them free of charge. *391 Orchard Road | MRT NS 22 Orchard or bus 7, 77 from Orchard Boulevard*

ROBINSONS THE HEEREN
(129 F5) (*🗺 G2*)
The new upmarket department store in the Robinsons chain offers fine wares from all over the globe and brands you'll find nowhere else in Singapore. Super-stylish displays. *260 Orchard Road | www.robinsons.com.sg | MRT NS 23 Somerset*

TANGLIN MALL (128 C4) (*🗺 E2*)
Wives of businessmen sent to Singapore from Western countries meet here in the morning for a cup of coffee and then go shopping. They know why: *Shopping*

at Tiffany's and *N's Boutique* sell INSIDER TIP designer clothing at outlet prices. *Daily 10am–9pm | 163 Tanglin Road | MRT NS 22 Orchard, then bus 7, 77, 123 from Orchard Boulevard*

INSIDER TIP **YUE HWA** (136 A3) (*🕮 H5*)
You can still feel the special charm of the 1980s in this Chinese department store behind the original facade – and it is only here, in the heart of Chinatown, that you will be able to find a fine selection of genuine silk underwear, *cheongsams* (Chinese dresses) and traditional Chinese medicine. *70 Eu Tong Sen Street | MRT NE 4, DT 19 Chinatown*

ELECTRONIC GOODS

If you prefer fixed prices, you should try the *Best Denki*, *Challenger* and *Harvey Norman* chains with many branches in the major shopping centres. Photo shops provide professional advice. Be careful about shopping in the *Orchard Towers* (129 D4) (*🕮 F1*) and *Lucky Plaza* (129 E4) (*🕮 F2*); you might get ripped off.

FUNAN IT MALL (136 B1–2) (*🕮 J4*)
The Funan IT Mall mainly focuses on customers looking for computer and camera accessories. *109 North Bridge Road | MRT EW 13, NS 25 City Hall*

LORDS CAMERAS AND WATCHES
(129 E4) (*🕮 F2*)
An exception in the Lucky Plaza: cameras at reasonable prices, with reliable service – but, do not forget to bargain. *304 Orchard Road | #01-79 Lucky Plaza | MRT NS 22 Orchard*

SIM LIM SQUARE
(130–131 C–D5) (*🕮 J2*)
Similar to the Funan IT Mall, this is a place where Singapore's computer experts like to shop. Sim Lim Square is a huge department store full of electronic shops from deep in the basement all the way up to the roof. As a rule, the prices here are fixed – but you can almost always manage to get a small discount. In 2015 a number of dealers were prosecuted and the police had to step in. *1 Rochor Canal Road | MRT EW 12 Bugis*

CLOTHING

You can buy international branded articles in all of the shopping centres and, naturally, on *Orchard* and *Scotts Roads*.

LOW BUDGET

Sports shoes, but also eyewear, are to be had at INSIDER TIP *Queensway Shopping Centre (1 Queensway/ Alexandra Road)* **(132 B2–3)** (*🕮* **A4**) at considerably lower prices than in the sports outlets in the city. Unique atmosphere: haggling is a must. Get there by taxi

Song & Song shops don't look good, but it's the price that counts. Where else can you find Adidas shirts for 15 S$ or Nike tennis skirts for 20 S$? Range on offer changes daily. E. g. *304 Orchard Road* **(129 E4)** (*🕮* **F2**) *(Lucky Plaza | MRT NS 22 Orchard), 245a Holland Av.* **(0)** (*🕮* **c4**) *(MRT CC 21 Holland Village)*

Bookworms do not always have to buy their books and newspapers. Just sit down for a browse at the huge book shop *Kinokuniya (391 Orchard Road | Ngee Ann City | #04–20B/C | MRT NS 22 Orchard)*.

The best places to buy cheap t-shirts are in the shops in *Little India* and in *Bugis Village (4 New Bugis Street | MRT EW 12, DT 14 Bugis)*. INSIDER TIP larger sizes can be found at *Marks & Spencer*, *Robinsons The Heeren*, *Metro* in the Paragon and in *Holland Road Shopping Centre*. Singapore promotes young design in a big way; fashion, too. Find out more about the local designers' often highly interesting labels at *www.yoursingapore.com/editorials/wear-it-local.html.*

BRITISH INDIA (137 D3–4) (*🗺 K–L5*)
Here, you can still feel all of the charm of colonial days. The brand with the elephant makes exquisite fashion with a touch of tropical apparel; it is expensive but some of the pieces are really original. *Sun–Thu 10am–11pm, Fri/Sat 10am–midnight | 2 Bayfront Av. | #B1–81 | The Shoppes at Marina Bay Sands | MRT CE 1, DT 16 Bayfront*

LOUIS VUITTON
(137 D3) (*🗺 K5*)
It is impossible to count all of the luxury shops in Singapore, but there is only one floating on the water. The French brand's flagship store can be reached through an underwater tunnel or over a bridge. There is a small bookshop selling the company's travel literature in the tunnel. *Sun–Thu 10am–11pm, Fri–Sat 10am–midnight | 2 Bayfront Av. | #B1–38/39, #B2–36/37/37 A | Crystal Pavilion North | MRT CE 1, DT 16 Bayfront*

ONG SHUNMUGAM (136 B4) (*🗺 J5*)
The award-winning Cheongsam designs (high-necked Chinese dresses) from this Singaporean atelier are not cheap, but worth every penny. *16 Raffles Quay | #B1–36 | Hong Leong Building | ongshunmugam.com | MRT EW 14, NS 26 Raffles Place*

SHANGHAI TANG
(129 E5) (*🗺 F–G2*)
The Singapore branch of the fashion chain from Shanghai has everything you can find in the main shop in China: expensive fashion with an exotic touch and the colours of Asia. Shanghai Tang was founded in 1994 by the Hong Kong businessman and playboy David Tang Wing-Cheung and regards itself as the first global lifestyle brand from the Middle Kingdom. *391 Orchard Road | #03–06/07 | Ngee Ann City | MRT NS 22 Orchard*

TONG TONG FRIENDSHIP STORE
(131 D6) (*🗺 K3*)
You'll find reasonably priced Chinese Cheongsams with a modern feel here, often with large, graphic patterns. The designer moves successfully between western and eastern styles. *100 Beach Road | #01–04 | Shaw Towers | www.tongtong.sg | MRT CC3 Esplanade*

ART & ANTIQUES

There are many shops where you can look and rummage around for something special on *South Bridge Road* (136 A3–4) (*🗺 H5*) and *Pagoda Street* (136 A3–4) (*🗺 H5*) in Chinatown. *Tanglin Shopping Centre* (129 D4) (*🗺 E1*) is also a good address for Buddha statues and South-East Asian art. The interessting new *National Design Centre* (131 D6) (*🗺 K3*) *(daily 9am–9pm | 111 Middle Road)* has changing exhibitions in an old colonial building.

ART PLURAL GALLERY (136 B1) (*🗺 J3*)
Swiss art dealer Frédéric de Senarclens opened one of the city's major modern-art galleries right in the heart of the museum district. Asian art and more. *38 Armenian Street | www.artpluralgallery.com | MRT EW 13, NS 25 City Hall*

GILLMAN BARRACKS (132 B5) *(🕮 A6)*
Singapore's art district could not be in a prettier location. A state-aided project sees 17 galleries housed in renovated barracks in the middle of the jungle. The guided tours and 'art after dark' events are real hits. Plus restaurant. *Tue–Sun noon–7pm, special events also till late | 9 Lock Road | www.gillmanbarracks.com | MRT CC 27 Labrador Park | bus 175 opposite Alexandra Point, stop no. 15 059*

RENAISSANCE ANTIQUE GALLERY (129 D4) *(🕮 E1)*
Fine, expensive collector's items from Myanmar and China. *Mon–Sat noon–6pm | 19 Tanglin Road | #02–32 | Tanglin Shopping Centre | www.tomlinson-collection.com | MRT NS 22 Orchard, then bus 36 from Orchard Boulevard*

TANGLIN SHOPPING CENTRE (129 D4) *(🕮 E1)*
Naga Arts and Antiques, Apsara and *Antiques of the Orient* have opened their doors in this shopping centre. *Antiques of the Orient* specialises not only in antiques but also in old maps and photographs. *19 Tanglin Road | MRT NS 22 Orchard, then bus 36 from Orchard Boulevard*

FURNITURE

It is also worth making a trip to Chinatown if you are looking for furniture. There are only a few genuine antiques – but even the reproduced cabinets can also be very attractive.

INSIDER TIP **JUST ANTHONY** (0) *(🕮 d3)*
An institution in Singapore: a large warehouse with restored Chinese furniture, as well as copies made using old wood; away from the centre. *Daily 9am–6.30pm | 379 Upper Paya Lebar Road | www.justanthony.com | MRT NE 12, CC 13 Serangoon, then bus 22, 43, 58*

INSIDER TIP **TAN BOON LIAT BUILDING** (134–135 C–D 2–3) *(🕮 F4)*
A good address with a large selection of old and reproduction furniture, acces-

Island of bags: Louis Vuitton resides on an island in Marina Bay

sories and carpets in a nondescript factory building. The *Journey East*, *Asia Passion*, *Red House*, *Eastern Discoveries* and *Fair Price Antiques* shops are worth a visit, but you'll have to bargain over the prices. *Daily from noon | 315 Outram Road | MRT EW 16, NE 3 Outram Park*

Oceans of silk in People's Park

TANGLIN VILLAGE (DEMPSEY HILL) ★ *(130 C4) (M 0)*
More and more restaurants are moving into the barracks on the former military base, but there are still some antique shops and galleries there. If you need a break during the process, there are plenty of good restaurants, cafés and wine bars in which you can relax. *Diagonally opposite the Singapore Botanic Gardens | MRT NS 22 Orchard/Orchard Boulevard | then bus 7, 77, 106, 123, 174*

TAILORS & FABRICS

Forget the 24-hour offers; you will only be annoyed later when you see the crooked seams and realise that what you bought does not really fit. Most of the tailors in the hotel arcades work swiftly and well. Prices for a high-quality suit start at around 500 S$ in Singapore. You will find the best selection of fabrics, including dazzling materials from India, silks and batiks, on *Arab Street* (131 D4–E5) *(M H2) (MRT EW 12, DT 14 Bugis)*

INSIDER TIP **CYC** (136 C1) *(M K3)*
Singapore's oldest shirt maker can satisfy the most demanding customers. You can buy not only the best men's shirts in town, but fashionable ladies' blouses, too. Prices start at 130 S$. The tailor will even be happy to renew collars and cuffs years later. *328 Newbridge Road | #02–12 | Raffles Hotel Arcade | MRT EW13, NS5 City Hall*

MUSTAFA ★ (131 D3) *(M K1)*
This gigantic, chaotic Indian department store is open around the clock. The cloth department is really special and there is usually a long queue of tailors waiting to be served. *320 Serangoon Road | www.mustafa.com.sg | MRT NE 8 Farrer Park*

INSIDER TIP **PEOPLE'S PARK** (135 F3) *(M H5)*
A place for real explorers: you can rummage around and haggle to your heart's content in the cloth market in Chinatown. Silk and batik can be tailored on the spot, and there are also small stands selling the most beautiful buttons. Many shops do not open until the afternoon. *100 Upper Cross Street | MRT NE 4, DT 19 Chinatown*

ROSSI (137 D1) *(M K3–4)*
Rossi has been part of Singapore's garment-making world for three generations.

However, tailoring the exquisite Italian fabric takes time. *9 Raffles Blvd. | #1–36 | Millenia Walk | tel. 63 34 18 00 | MRT CC 4, DT 15 Promenade*

SOUVENIRS

Colourfully painted wood carvings of fruit and animals, stick puppets from Indonesia, pewter goods from Malaysia and Chinese seal stamps, porcelain figures, place mats and jade in all forms can be found in the many small shophouses in Chinatown. Herbal teas also make popular souvenirs. Little India, with Arab Street and Bugis, is a treasure trove for souvenir-hunters.

CHOCOLATE RESEARCH FACILITY
(137 D1) *(K3–4)*
Are you friends fond of chocolate with Sichuan pepper or black sesame? Get it here, in a shop that does'nt look anything like a sweet shop, but has the white-tiled atmosphere of a laboratory. The (expensive) blocks of chocolate are attractively wrapped and make a fine souvenir. There are more than 100 different varieties to choose from. *252 North Bridge Road | #B1-49 Raffles City | MRT NS 25, EW 13 Cityhall*

EU YANG SAN (136 A4) *(H5)*
This shop for traditional Chinese herbal medicine was already founded in 1879. *269 South Bridge Road | MRT NE 4, DT 19 Chinatown*

LITTLE INDIA ARCADE (130 C4) *(J2)*
This market is brimming with fabrics, pashminas, fashion jewellery as well as Indian needlework. There's sure to be something unusual here to take home with you. The INSIDER TIP henna tattoos, painted freehand on the skin, are cheap and particularly beautiful. *48 Serangoon Road | MRT NE 7 Little India*

PRINTS (129 E4) *(F2)*
You are in Singapore and discover that your diary is almost full. No problem! Go to Prints; they can help you with their incredible selection. The small shop has the most beautiful diaries and notebooks, photo albums and pocket calendars – but, they are not exactly cheap. E. g. *ION Orchard | 2 Orchard Turn | #04–26 | www.prints-international.com | MRT NS 22 Orchard*

RAFFLES HOTEL SHOP
(136 C1) *(K3)*
The shop in the exclusive Raffles Hotel sells tasteful, but rather pricey, souvenirs. *1 Beach Road | MRT EW 13, NS 5 City Hall*

RISIS
Would you like to take some Singapore orchids home with you and have them live forever? Then, *Risis* is just the right place for you: this is where you can buy Singapore's national flower plated with gold. Branches: *Singapore Botanic Gardens* (128 A2) *(C1) (Cluny Road | MRT NS 22 Orchard | then bus 7, 77, 106 from Orchard Boulevard), C. K. Tangs* department store (129 E4) *(F2) (310 Orchard Road | #B1–17 | MRT NS 22 Orchard)*

ROYAL SELANGOR
(137 D3–4) *(K–L5)*
The traditional pewter studio was founded in Kuala Lumpur in Malaysia. After years of only selling dusty tankards and kitsch, Australian designers spruced up the programme. E. g. *10 Bayfront Av. | #B2–92 | Marina Bay Sands | www.royalselangor.com | MRT CE 1 Bayfront*

SIFR AROMATICS (131 E5) *(K2)*
The place to buy perfumed oils in a huge range of scents, produced by this Singaporean institution. A very special souvenir. *42 Arab Street | MRT EW 12, DT 14 Bugis*

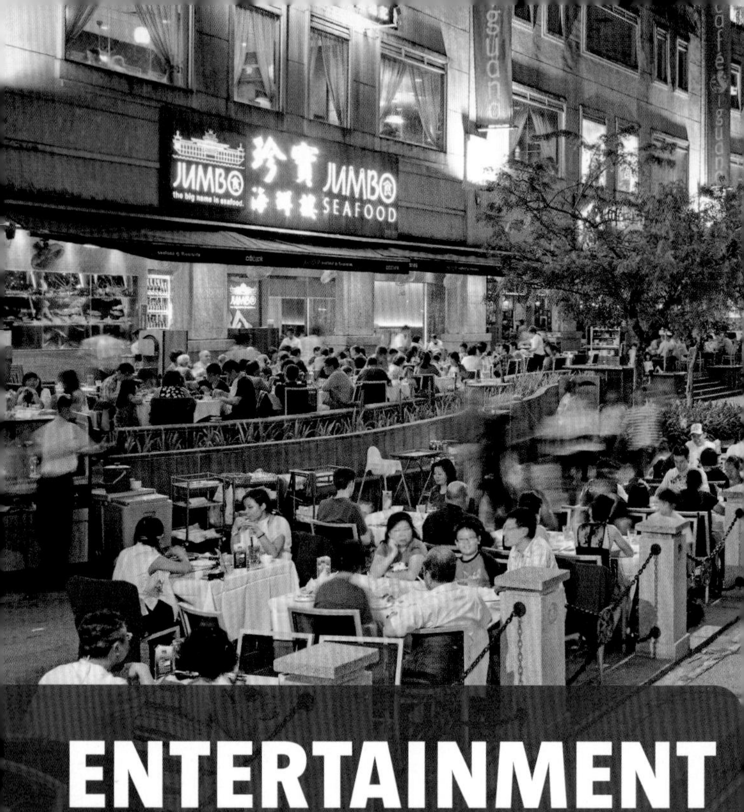

ENTERTAINMENT

> **WHERE TO START?**
> The bad news to begin with – you will have to make a choice. The good news: it is impossible to make a wrong decision – you can find everything you are looking for. You should start at the **rooftop terrace of the Fullerton Bay Hotel (136 C3)** *(J–K5)*: and then head for one of the many nearby nightspots. There is a risk that you will not feel like moving on, however. Many people have spent more than half the evening up here.

Years ago, the name of the city had a certain double meaning attached to it – many people called Singapore 'sin galore'.

That all changed when the city state became independent in 1965. The new government cleaned things up, introduced censorship, made drug dealing a capital offence, and broke up criminal rings. This made the city one of the safest in the world. However, many visitors and locals then found it rather boring. That is no longer true. By the first night-time Formula 1 race in 2009, Singapore had begun to show what it is really capable of: a tropical metropolis that rocks, one that turns balmy

Photo: Party zone: Clarke Quay

Non-stop fun: swinging Singapore is well on the way to becoming a globally fashionable party capital

evenings into long nights and where everybody finds what they are looking for once the sun goes down! After a few false starts, the government has managed to cast off its image of being a bit of a wet blanket. The new tourists and gamblers in the casino generate income. This led to the birth of the concept of 'Swinging Singapore'. The concept is bearing fruit: new bars, pubs and clubs are shooting up all over town. Today, Singapore also offers a wide range of cultural activities. Information on events is given in the local press such as the *Straits Times*. *Timeout* magazine is even better and can be bought at all newsstands. The city has a large number of bar and amusement districts, which attract very different groups. The city's flashiest – and sometimes overpriced – entertainment area is around

Brewed in the house: Brewerkz

Boat Quay (136 B–C 2–3) (*H4–5*). The in-crowd now tends to meet a few hundred yards further upstream at ★ *Clarke Quay* (136 A2) (*H4*) and *Robertson Quay* (135 D2) (*G4*). The more mature prefer the bars, pubs and restaurants in *Tanglin Village (Dempsey Hill)* (128 A4–5) (*C2*). The former barracks provide a mix of rustic charm and haute cuisine in the shade of tropical trees. Singapore's youth lets their hair down in the bars along *Mohamed Sultan Road* (135 E1–2) (*G4*) until well after midnight. The area around *Duxton Road* (135 E–F5) (*H6*) in Chinatown and nearby *Club Street* (135 F4) (*H5*) is the preferred stomping ground for the city's nouveau riche crowd and expats. *Kampong Glam* and *Little India* are becoming increasingly attractive with the experimental and alternative scene.

The cafés around *Emerald Hill* (129 F5) (*G2*) on Orchard Road mainly attract tourists. The former *Chijmes Monastery* (130 C6) (*J3*), with its restaurants and bars, on the other hand is popular with locals and tourists alike. The venerable Raffles Hotel (136 C1) (*K3*), with the *Long Bar* is directly opposite. This is where the *Singapore Sling*, the country's national cocktail, was mixed for the first time in 1915. Today, it tastes better in some of the other bars – but the atmosphere of the Long Bar still makes it worth visiting.

BARS & PUBS

Happy hour makes the high prices in the centrally located pubs a little more tolerable. Some establishments reduce the prices for individual drinks but the 2-for-1 principle, where you get two glasses of beer or wine for the price of one, is more common (usually 5–8pm).

1-ALTITUDE ★

(136 B3) (*J5*)

Dance 282m (925ft) above the sea: from this vantage point, the whole city lies spread out at your feet. You can enjoy the good music and wide choice of cool drinks at the same time. No shorts allowed. On the floor below, you can perfect your drive at the indoor golf course. *Mon–Thu 6pm–1am, Fri/Sat 6pm–3am | admission fees vary | 1 Raffles Place | # 63 | www.1-altitude.com | MRT NS 26, EW 14 Raffles Place*

28 HONGKONG STREET
(136 A–B 2–3) (📖 H4)
Hip bar behind a nondescript façade. The barkeeper is known far and wide for his brilliant cocktails; style reminiscent of Manhattan. *Mon–Thu 5.30pm–1am, Fri/Sat 5.30pm–3am | 28 Hongkong Street | www.28hks.com | MRT NE 5 Clarke Quay*

INSIDER TIP **BAR STORIES**
(131 E5) (📖 K2)
Chocolate with cucumber juice and champagne? No problem. The barman here will mix any cocktail you want. *Sun–Tue noon–8pm, Wed–Sat noon–1am | 55/57a Haji Lane | MRT EW 12, DT 14 Bugis*

BREWERKZ
(135 F2) (📖 H4)
Large pub-restaurant with a micro-brewery to guarantee that only fresh beer is served. It tastes great and is less expensive than in many other pubs. *Mon–Thu noon–1am, Fri–Sat noon–3am, Sun 11am–1am | 30 Merchant Road | #01–05 | Riverside Point | MRT NE 5 Clarke Quay*

KINKI ROOF TOP BAR
(136 B–C4) (📖 J5)
If the roof terrace at the Fullerton Bay Hotel too expensive and starchy, you'll love it here: the view over Marina Bay is the same, but the guests are younger, and graffiti adorns the walls. *Mon–Thu 5pm–midnight, Fri/Sat 5pm–open end | 70 Collyer Quay | #02–02 | www.kinki.com.sg | MRT NS 26, EW 14 Raffles Place*

CLUBS & DISCOTHEQUES

There are so many discos in Singapore that some are empty from Sunday to Thursday. On these days, the prices, which usually include one drink, are not as high. However, most are packed at the weekend, and often members-only late on.

AVALON AND PANGAEA ★
(137 D3–4) (📖 K5)
Two highlights under one glass roof: two floors on Marina Bay. Dance on a floating platform at *Avalon*; the *Pangaea* is the place to chill out. *Wed, Fri–Sun 10pm–6am | 2 Bayfront Av. | South Crystal Pavilion | www.avalon.sg | MRT CE 1, DT 16 Bayfront*

THE BUTTER FACTORY
(136 C3) (📖 K5)
Located directly on Marina Bay, this club offers a mix of hip-hop, urban grooves and electro-sound on several floors. When you

MARCO POLO HIGHLIGHTS

★ Clarke Quay
The best place to go out and have fun on the Singapore River → p. 84

★ 1-Altitude
The highest open-air bar → p. 84

★ Avalon
Chic and expensive: the floating club in Marina Bay is the place to be seen → p. 85

★ Cocoon
Indulge yourself protected by terracotta guards → p. 86

★ Zouk
Singapore's most famous discotheque → p. 87

★ Esplanade
Culture for all tastes in South-East Asia's largest concert house → p. 88

have had you fill of dancing, you can admire the view of the water or take a morning stroll along the Singapore River. *Wed 11pm–4am, Fri/Sat 11pm–5am | 1 Fullerton Road | #02–02/03/04 | One Fullerton | www.thebutterfactory.com | MRT NS 26 EW 14 Raffles Place*

INSIDER TIP **CANVAS** (136 B2) *(🗺 J4)*
This club aims to unite art, fashion and music. Performers include local artists such as drag queen Kumar. *Tue 3pm–midnight, Wed/Thu 3pm–2am, Fri 3pm–3am, Sat 9pm–4am | 20 Upper Circular Road | #B1–01 | www.canvasvenue.sg | MRT NE 5 Clarke Quay*

CHAMÄLEON CLUB (0) *(🗺 B1)*
Under tropical trees in an old colonial building in the busy watering-hole Dempsey Hill. There's a dance floor above the bar with some spectacular lighting. The house cocktail is the 'Rockstar'. *Wed, Fri/Sat 7pm–open end | 22 Dempsey Road | MRT NS 22 Orchard, then bus 7, 77, 123,174 from Orchard Boulevard*

COCOON ★ (136 A2) *(🗺 H4)*
Another coup for the IndoChine Group: enormous terracotta sentinels guard the entrance that leads to the Cocoon Bar on the ground floor and *Madame Butterfly Restaurant* upstairs. Opulence with opium couches, silk cushions and crystal chandeliers. *Sun–Thu 3pm–3am, Fri/Sat 3pm–6am | Merchant's Court | 3a River Valley Road | #01–02 | indochine-group.com | MRT NE 5 Clarke Quay*

DBL O (131 D5–6) *(🗺 K2)*
The *double O* dazzles with four bars, a large dance floor and a lot of light. One of the biggest dance clubs in the city. *Tue–Fri 6pm–3am, Sat 6pm–4am | 222 Queen*

BOOKS & FILMS

Singapore – A Biography – the book by Mark Ravinder Frost and Yu-Mei Balasingamchow is a wonderful kaleidoscope of the history of the city state

12 Storeys – the Singaporean director Eric Khoo Kim Hai's films provides a fascinating, somewhat satirical, view of life in the government-subsidised housing of the average person in the city (1997). Khoo's film 'Be with Me' was presented at the 2005 Cannes Festival

Singapore Shophouses – Julian Davison and Luca Invernizzi Tettoni have put together a fascinating book on this building form. Author Julian Davison traces the history of shophouses, which Tettoni illustrates beautifully with his photographs.

I not stupid – has become a legendary saying in the city state. The critical filmmaker Jack Neo Chee Keong takes an analytical look at Singapore society in this work (2002)

In the Footsteps of Stamford Raffles – this updated version of the book on the life and times of the founder of Singapore Sir Stamford Raffles (1781–1826) by British ethnologist Nigel Barley was published in 2010

Almayer's Folly – Joseph Conrad's travel tale of a European in colonial Singapore

Zouk, superlative dance floor: three discos, international DJs, always packed

Street | # 01–01/02 | www.dbl-o.com | MRT CC 2 Bras Basah

DREAM UND FENIX ROOM
(136 A–B2) *(🕮 H4)*
Taiwanese-American entrepreneur John Langan has shown once again what he's capable of: the *Dream* is a disco, which combines beats and videos; the *Fenix Room* its glamorous club counterpart. It reminds you of the lounges of the legendary 1920s. Large selection of champagne. *Wed–Sat 9.30pm–open end | River Valley Road | Block 3c | MRT NE 5 Clarke Quay*

HELIPAD (135 F2) *(🕮 H4)*
This is the home of the 'Flying Sarong' drink and much, much more: The lounge is on the rooftop helipad of a house on Clarke Quay. The 'Helipad Ice Tea' consists of a potent mix of many ingredients – but not a lot of tea. *Daily noon–2am | 6 Eu Tong Sen Street | #05–22 | The Central | www.helipad.com.sg | MRT NE 5 Clarke Quay*

INSIDER TIP **TIMBRE@SUBSTATION AND TIMBRE@THE ARTS HOUSE**
Many local groups preform on the stage in the garden at *Timbre @ Substation* (136 B1) *(🕮 J3) (Sun–Thu 6pm–1am, Fri/Sat 6pm–2am | 45 Armenian Street | The Substation Garden | MRT CC 2 Bras Basah)*, an independent culture centre. Offshoot *Timbre@The Arts House* (136 B2) *(🕮 J4) (Mon–Thu 6pm–1am, Fri/Sat 6pm–2am | 1 Old Parliament Lane/High Street | MRT EW 13, NS 25 City Hall)* is located on the Singapore River, next to the Parliament, with an open-air stage. *www.timbregroup.asia/timbresg*

ZOUK ★ (135 D2) *(🕮 F4)*
Singapore's best known disco is always full and attracts famous DJs from all over the world. In three warehouses there are three discos featuring different music styles: *Zouk (Wed, Fri/Sat 10pm–open end), Phuture (Wed, Fri/Sat 9pm–open end)* and *Velvet Underground (Wed, Fri/Sat 9pm–open end). 17 Jiak Kim Street | www.zoukclub.com | MRT NE 5 Clarke Quay*

CINEMA

The Singaporeans are great film fans. There are cinemas on the upper floors of many of the shopping centres on *Orchard Road*, in *Vivo City* and in the renovated, Art Deco theatre *The Cathay*. There is a complicated classification system with the advisory ratings *G* (general) *PG* (parental guidance) and *PG13* (not recommended for children under 13) and age restrictions *NC16* (no children) and *M18* (only for mature audiences). Cinema programme at *movies.insing.com*

CONCERTS, THEATRE, BALLET

There are performances of classical and modern plays, concerts, musicals and ballet every day of the week. Most take place in *Esplanade* (136 C2) (*K4*). The painstakingly restored *Victoria Theatre and Concert Hall* (136 B2) (*J4*) *(11 Empress Place)* is an attractive venue. Tickets for most cultural events are sold by the central ticketing service *sistic (e. g. | Mon–Sat 10am–8pm, Sun noon–8pm | 313 Orchard Road | #B1, Concierge Counter | 313@Somerset | ticket hotline 63 48 55 55 | www.sistic.com.sg | MRT NS 23 Somerset)*.

LOW BUDGET

Those who are after rock music head for the *Esplanade* **(136 C2)** (***K4***) *(www.esplanade.com | bus 77, 171, 174, 36)*. No, you will not have to fork out 100 dollars for a ticket. Singapore's rock musicians get together for a free session on the open-air stage behind the building directly on the water *(Fri–Sun 7.30–10pm)*.

Singapore's latest favourite pastime has a very romantic touch to it: illuminated kites circle over the Singapore River. As long as it is not raining, you can watch this aerial art at Riverside Point opposite Clarke Quay **(135 F2)** (***H4***) *(bus 12, 33 | MRT NE 5 Clarke Quay, then on foot)*.

CHINESE STREET OPERA

(135 F4) (*H5*)

Stages made of bamboo scaffolding and tarpaulins are put up on the streets on festive occasions (especially during the Festival of the Hungry Spirits). That is when the opera stars in their spectacular costumes and elaborate make-up recount legends from China's history in their shrill falsetto voices for hours on end. If you happen to be in Singapore when there is no Chinese festival, you can still get a taste of China's operatic art: every Friday and Saturday evening, the *Chinese Theatre Circle (Fri/Sat 7pm–9pm | admission incl. dinner 40 S$ | 5 Smith Street | tel. 63 23 48 62 | www.ctcopera.com.sg | MRT NE 4 Chinatown)*, a traditional Chinese troupe, performs popular Cantonese operas in its tea house in Chinatown.

CONCERTS

The Singapore Symphony Orchestra was founded in 1979 and has given more or less regular performances on Friday and Saturday nights since then. You can obtain information on concerts from ★ *Esplanade* (136 C2) (*K4*) *(www.esplanade.com)* or at *www.sso.org.sg*. The *Esplanade* is also the venue of many guest performances by international soloists and orchestras. Concerts also take place on Sundays on the INSIDER TIP *Shaw Foundation Symphony*

Stage in a romantic setting in Singapore's old Botanic Gardens (128 A2) (🕮 O) *(www.sbg.org.sg)*, including jazz, classical and occasionally pop music. From time to time, music festivals are organised in *Fort Canning Park* (136 A–B 1–2) (🕮 H–J 3–4) and more intimate concerts are also presented in the *Jubilee Hall* of Raffles Hotel (136 C1) (🕮 K3). The INSIDER TIP *Nanyang Academy of Fine Arts*

Legends from the Middle Kingdom: Chinese street operas are a unique experience

(tel. 65 12 40 00 | www.nafu.edu.sg) organises regular performances of classical Chinese music. If you are interested in Indian music and dance performances, you should consult the INSIDER TIP *Singapore Indian Fine Arts Society (tel. 62 99 59 29 | www.sifas.org)*.

INSIDER TIP LAUGH WITH KUMAR

Singapore's top drag-queen makes fun of the government and everything close to Singaporean hearts. Kumar can get away with more than anybody else. He performs in various places across the city, but puts in regular appearances at the *Hard Rock Café* (129 D4) (🕮 E2) *(shows: Sat 11pm–1am | 50 Cuscaden Road | #04–01 | HPL House | book tickets in advance under tel. 62 35 52 32 | MRT NS 22 Orchard)*.

THEATRE

Theatrical performances in Singapore continue to be subject to government censorship. Fans of experimental theatre should visit the *Action Theatre* (130 C6) (🕮 J3) *(42 Waterloo Street | tel. 68 37 08 42 | MRT EW 12 Bugis | www.action.org.sg)* in a restored pre-war bungalow, or *The Substation* (136 B1) (🕮 J3) *(45 Armenian Street | tel. 63 37 75 35 | www.substation.org | MRT NS 25, EW 13 City Hall | MRT CC 2 Bras Basah, then bus 197)*. Currently, the best English-language stage in Singapore is the *Singapore Repertory Theatre* (135 E2) (🕮 H4) *(DBS Arts Centre | 20 Merbau Road | tel. 67 33 81 66 | www.srt.com.sg | MRT NE 5 Clarke Quay)*

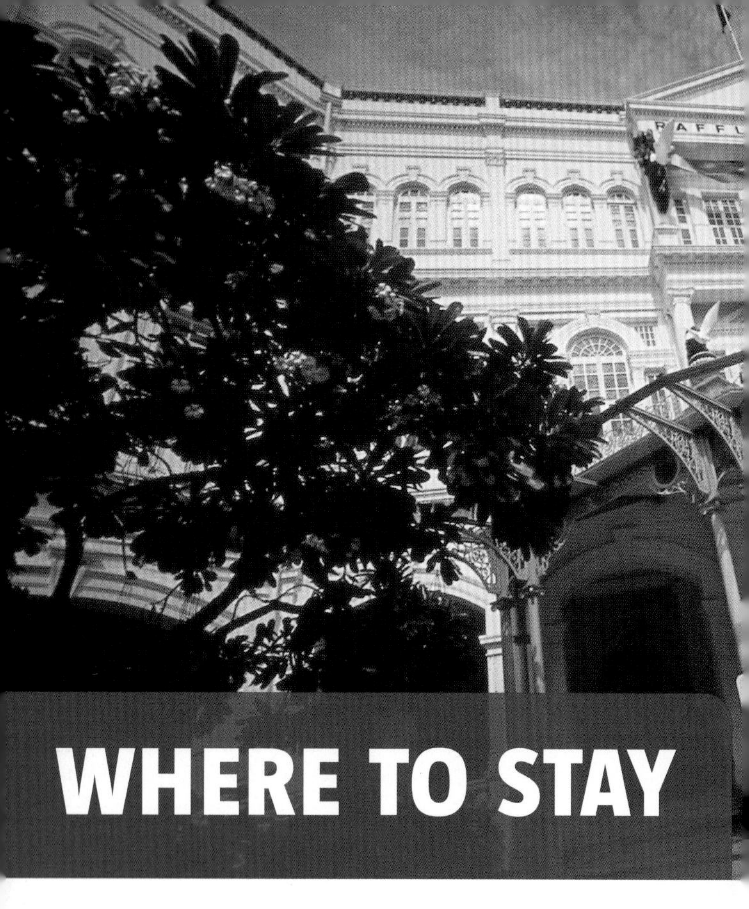

WHERE TO STAY

There is an almost endless choice of first-class hotels in Singapore. The Marina Bay Sands Casino and Congress Complex alone has more than 2500 beds. Five hotels – including Singapore's first Hard Rock Hotel – have opened their doors near the other casino on Sentosa.

You can live in a colonial building as guests do in elegant Raffles, in small designer hotels created in former Chinese shop-houses like The Scarlet or in charming homes away from home on the beach, such as The Capella.

The city has also now started to encourage backpacker hotels, in order to appeal to this kind of tourist, too. In principle: the further the hotel is away from the tourist areas and the shopping centres, the lower the price. Since bus, MRT and taxi fares are low, it is an option worth consideration.

If Singapore is a break in your flight to Bali or Australia, ask your travel agent or airline about stopover hotels; that can bring a reduction of up to 50 percent. In addition, the *Singapore Hotel Association* operates a counter at Changi Airport that is open 24 hours a day and organises last-minute rooms at reduced rates in hotels that are not fully booked. You can also contact hotels in the Internet via *www.stayinginsingapore.com.sg.*

 Photo: Raffles Hotel

Accommodation in a shophouse? Charming, reasonably priced hotels are now vying with the ultramodern luxury establishments

HOTELS: EXPENSIVE

FAIRMONT SINGAPORE/ SWISSÔTEL THE STAMFORD

(136 C1) (J3)

The two high-rise hotels *Fairmont (80 Bras Basah Road | tel. 63 39 77 77 | www.fairmont.com)* and *The Stamford (2 Stamford Road | tel. 63 38 85 85 | www. swissotel.com)* built on top of the Raffles City shopping centre together have a total of 2049 rooms. The taller tower houses the Swissôtel The Stamford. The view from the rooms on the upper floors over the city and islands is spectacular. The hotels have a total of 16 restaurants between them; right at the top are the *Jaan* and the *Equinox*. *www.rafflescity hotels.com | MRT NS 25, EW 13 City Hall, CC 3 Esplanade*

'Lobbying' in the 1929 in Chinatown

INTERCONTINENTAL 131 D6) *(🕮 J–K3)*
The hotel belongs to the retail and office complex Bugis Junction. Top levels of comfort in this somewhat expensive shophouse accommodation give you a sense of the Singapore of old. *406 rooms | 80 Middle Road | Bugis Junction | tel. 63 38 76 00 | www.intercontinental.com | MRT EW 12, DT 14 Bugis*

INSIDER TIP **NAUMI** (131 D6) *(🕮 K3)*
The luxury boutique hotel in the shade of its large predecessor, Raffles, has only 40 suites. But they've really got what it takes: each is individually decorated, and for your morning workout each room has a yoga mat and a selection of electronic 'toys' such as Xbox or Wii to choose from. A butler is on hand around the clock. Service is writ large at the Naumi – after all, it's one of the best small hotels in the world. *41 Seah Street | tel. 6 43 60 00 | www.naumihotel.com | MRT NS 25, EW 13 City Hall | MRT CC 3 Esplanade*

NEW MAJESTIC HOTEL ★
(135 E4) *(🕮 G6)*
When the lawyer Loh Lik Peng discovered that he had no more room in his home for his furniture collection, he renovated a dilapidated house in Chinatown, turned it into a hotel and had its 30 rooms decorated by Asian designers. *31–37 Bukit Pasoh Road | tel. 65 11 47 00 | www.newmajestichotel.com | MRT EW 16, NE 3 Outram Park*

PARKROYAL ON PICKERING
(136 A3) *(🕮 H5)*
Situated between Chinatown, the financial district and the pubs and clubs on the Singapore River, this new hotel is a green oasis, welcoming guests with hanging gardens outside. Relax after your shopping spree in the prize-winning spa, *St. Gregory*. *367 rooms | 3 Upper Pickering Street | tel. 68 09 88 88 | www.parkroyalhotels.com/en/hotels-resorts/singapore/pickering.html | MRT NE 4, DT 19 Chinatown*

ROYAL PLAZA ON SCOTTS
(129 E4) *(🕮 F1)*
You couldn't stay more centrally in Singapore's shopping district. Although not as charming as others in the city, the hotel is functional and reasonably priced for its location. With swimming pool. *511 rooms | 25 Scotts Road | tel. 67 37 79 66 | MRT NS 22 Orchard | www.royalplaza.com.sg*

HOTELS: MODERATE

1929 ★ (135 E4) *(🕮 H5)*
This house is the less expensive sister of the New Majestic Hotel. Accommodation here, too, is in a restored building in the

heart of Chinatown, with chic, designer-furnished rooms. The 1929, however, has no pool. *32 rooms | 50 Keong Saik Road | tel. 63 47 19 29 | www.hotel1929.com | MRT EW 16, NE 3 Outram Park | MRT NE 4, DT 19 Chinatown*

COPTHORNE KING'S HOTEL, FURAMA RIVERFRONT, HOLIDAY INN ATRIUM, MIRAMAR, RIVER VIEW
(135 D2) (*G4*)
These five hotels located close to each other in the Clarke Quay pub district, but far away from Singapore's shopping and business streets, have a total of 1965 rooms. That means that the prices for an overnight stay are fairly reasonable considering the comfort they offer. With the exception of the Furama Riverfront, all the hotels have a swimming pool. *Copthorne King's Hotel (403 Havelock Road | tel. 67 33 00 11 | wwwcopthornekings.com.sg), Furama Riverfront (405 Havelock Road | tel. 63 33 88 98), Holiday Inn Atrium (317 Outram Road | tel. 67 33 01 88 | www.holiday-inn.com), Miramar (401 Havelock Road | tel. 67 33 02 22 | www.miramar.com.sg), River View (382 Havelock Road | tel. 67 32 99 22 | www.riverview.com.sg). MRT NE 5 Clarke Quay, then bus 51*

GALLERY HOTEL ★ (135 E2) (*G4*)
Singapore's first boutique hotel. A colourful spot in the heart of the fashionable Clarke Quay district with a spectacular pool on the roof. *223 rooms | 1 Nanson Road | tel. 68 49 86 86 | www.galleryhotel.com.sg | MRT NE 5 Clarke Quay, then bus 51*

HOLIDAY INN EXPRESS CLARKE QUAY
(135 E2) (*H4*)
New hotel from the chain includes breakfast and wi-fi. It may stand at a junction, but it is right in Singapore's entertainment district on the Singapore River. *442 rooms | 2 Magazine Road | tel. 65 89 80 00 | www.ihg.com | MRT NE 5 Clarke Quay*

PERAK HOTEL (131 D4) (*J2*)
This charming small hotel and guesthouse in a renovated Peranakan house in Little

MARCO POLO HIGHLIGHTS

★ New Majestic Hotel
Created by a design collector for design fans: where the hotel room is a showcase → p. 92

★ 1929
Youthful chic in an old shophouse in Chinatown → p. 92

★ Gallery Hotel
In the fashionable Clarke Quay area and extremely stylish all the way up to the swimming pool on the roof → p. 93

★ The Scarlet
Small but very elegant – and that in the middle of Chinatown → p. 94

★ Capella Singapore
Reside in elegance on the beach on Sentosa → p. 94

★ Raffles Hotel
A magnificent resurrection: the institution among Singapore's hotels → p. 94

★ Adler Hostel
Princely accommodation for the tight budget. Singapore's first luxury hostel → p. 95

★ YMCA International House
Not really a youth hostel but a good hotel at a giveaway price → p. 97

India is tastefully decorated. It is privately run and the friendly staff are happy to give tips about all of the things to be discovered in the neighbourhood. *34 rooms | 12 Perak Road | tel. 62 99 77 33 | www.peraklodge.net | MRT NE 7, DT 12 Little India*

THE SCARLET ★ (135 F4) (*🕮 H6*)
The location in the heart of Chinatown is great; the decoration breathtaking: the red brocade and opulent gold and black create a Baroque atmosphere, the porters wear livery. The shophouses along an entire street were connected and renovated to create this hotel. *5 suites, 79 rooms | 33 Erskine Road | tel. 65 11 33 33 | www.thescarlethotel.com | MRT NE 4, DT 19 Chinatown*

SILOSO BEACH RESORT
(138 B4) (*🕮 P6*)
Fancy staying a little outside the city? Why not try the seaside promenade on the leisure island of Sentosa? The resort is the

LUXURY HOTELS

Capella Singapore ★
(138–139 C–D5) (*🕮 Q7*)
It cannot get more beautiful than this. The colonial building that was extended by Norman Foster has a panoramic view across the open sea. The rooms and restaurant facilities are first-class. *116 rooms, suites, apts. | from 500 S$ | Sentosa Island | from Vivo City (MRT CC 29, NE 1 HarbourFront) with the Sentosa Express (S2 Imbiah) or by bus; pick-up service is available | tel. 63 77 88 88 | www.capellasingapore.com*

The Fullerton (136 C3) (*🕮 J5*)
This luxurious hotel is in an old colonial building on Boat Quay. *400 rooms from 450 S$, suites up to 6000 S$ | 1 Fullerton Square | tel. 67 33 83 88 | www.fullertonhotel.com | MRT NS 26, EW 14 Raffles Place*

Marina Bay Sands Hotel
(137 D3–4) (*🕮 K–L5*)
This establishment with its three towers has no need to advertise: you already know the rooftop pool from thousands of photos seen around the world. It is located in what is actually a city in the city – including the largest casino in south-east Asia – and within walking distance of the new Botanic Gardens. You do not actually need to leave it at all during your stay in Singapore. *2560 rooms from 350 S$ | 10 Bayfront Av. | tel. 66 88 88 97 | www.marinabaysands.com | MRT CE 1, DT 16 Bayfront*

Raffles Hotel ★ (136 C1) (*🕮 K3*)
This legendary hotel is even more luxurious since its magnificent refurbishment. *104 suites from 650–6000 S$ | 1 Beach Road | tel. 63 37 18 86 | www.raffles.com | MRT NS 25, EW 13 City Hall*

Shangri-La (128–129 C–D3) (*🕮 E1*)
In its advertisements, the hotel neither focuses especially on its excellent service, nor even on the *High Tea* served on the *Rose Veranda*; its pride and joy is the landscaped garden. *760 rooms from 375 S$, suites up to 3200 S$ | 22 Orange Grove Road | tel. 67 37 36 44 | www.shangri-la.com | MRT NS 22 Orchard, then by taxi or walk*

The renovated Fullerton Hotel has preserved its Classicist façade

only one in Singapore with a spring-fed landscape pool and does all it can to protect natural resources. *182 rooms | 51 Imbiah Walk | tel. 67 22 33 33 | www.silosobeachresort.com | MRT S3 Beach (Sentosa)*

THE SULTAN (131 E4–5) *(⊞ J2)*
Stepping out at The Sultan: ten old colonial houses were combined to make this hotel, which boasts the *Singjazz Club* and *Wonderbar* in the new trendy district Kampong Glam. *64 rooms | 101 Jalan Sultan | tel. 67 23 71 01 | www.thesultan.com.sg | MRT EW 12, DT 14 Bugis*

VILLAGE HOTEL ALBERT COURT
(130 C4) *(⊞ J2)*
Small, cosy hotel near Little India, known for its friendly atmosphere. *136 rooms | 180 Albert Street | tel. 63 39 39 39 | www.stayfareast.com | MRT NE 7 Little India*

VILLAGE HOTEL BUGIS
(131 E5) *(⊞ K2)*
Most of the 393 rooms have a fine view of the old Malay district. The hotel is in the programmes of numerous touroperators. It has a swimming pool and also extremely competitive prices, as it is located quite a way from the major shopping streets. *390 Victoria Street | tel. 62 97 28 28 | www.stayfareast.com | MRT EW 12 Bugis*

INSIDER TIP **WANDERLUST**
(130 C4) *(⊞ G1)*
Four renowned Singaporean designers and architects pooled their talents to create this gem out of what was once a schoolhouse. The ultramodern boutique hotel is in the heart of Little India, the liveliest district in the tropical metropolis. *29 rooms | 2 Dickson Road | tel. 63 96 33 22 | www.wanderlusthotel.com | MRT NE 7 DT 12 Little India | MRT DT 22 Jln Besar*

HOTELS: BUDGET

ADLER HOSTEL ★ (135 F3) *(⊞ H5)*
A hostel, but a prize-winning, luxurious one. It is located in a renovated shophouse in the centre of Chinatown and

is furnished with antqiue furniture and local arts and crafts. *2 dormitories with 16 beds each | 259 South Bridge Road | tel. 62 26 01 73 | www.adlerhostel.com | MRT NE 4, DT 19 Chinatown*

INSIDER TIP HANGOUT@MT.EMILY

(130 B4) (*M H2*)

The modern but inexpensive lodge received an award from Singapore's tourism authority. The rooms are air-conditioned and have private bathrooms; the dormitories have beds for five to seven guests. One special point is that the operators donate one dollar of the room price to charity organisations. The *Wild Rocket Restaurant (www.wildrocket.com.sg)* in the same building serves modern, light Singaporean cuisine. *54 rooms | 10 A Upper Wilkie Road | tel. 64 38 55 88 | www.hangout-hotels.com | MRT CC 1, NE 6, NS 24 Dhoby Ghaut, then bus 64, 65, 139*

LOW BUDGET

It is not absolutely essential to stay in a hotel in Singapore. You can even pitch a tent in this tropical metropolis – and it is completely free of charge in the *East Coast Park* **(0)** ***(M O–S3)****(tel. 180 04 71 73 00 | www.nparks.gov.sg | bus 16 to Marine Terrace, then through the underpass to the East Coast Park | www.nparks.gov.sg)*. There, you just have to set up the tent you brought with you and a park attendant will come along and take down your particulars.

Nice-sounding name and cheap beds in the dormitory: the *Betel Box* **(138 A5)** ***(M R1)*** *(200 Joo Chiat Road | tel. 62 47 73 40 | www.betelbox.com | CC 9, EW 8 Paya Lebar)*. The hostel in the Peranakan district Katong offers simple beds from 20 S$. Family rooms cost 80 S$.

ROBERTSON QUAY HOTEL

(135 E2) (*M H4*)

The building is not especially attractive from the outside, but it is in a fine location directly in Singapore's amusement area and even has a rooftop pool. Orchard Road and the commercial districts are also just a short distance away. *150 rooms | 15 Merbau Road | tel. 67 35 33 33 | www.robertsonquayhotel.com.sg | MRT NE 5 Clarke Quay*

INSIDER TIP THE ROYAL PEACOCK

(135 E4) (*M G–H6*)

The 73 rooms and six suites are hidden in a renovated row of houses in the heart of Chinatown. Located in what was once the city's red-light district, the Peacock is now surrounded by bars and restaurants. *55 Keong Saik Road | tel. 62 23 35 22 | www.royalpeacockhotel.com | MRT EW 16, NE 3 Outram Park*

SANTA GRAND HOTEL EAST COAST

(138 B6) (*M S1*)

This modest hotel in the heart of Katong, the colourful, traditional quarter outside the city centre of Singapore, offers you good value for money. The hotel's own Peranakan restaurant rates as one of the best in town. *73 rooms | 171 East Coast Road | tel. 63 44 68 66 | www.santagrandhotels.com | MRT EW 8, CC 9 Paya Lebar, then bus 40*

STRAND (130 C6) (*M J3*)

The 130 functionally equipped rooms have televisions with a video programme; there is also a lounge with live music and a coffee shop. Excellent location in the centre of town. *25 Bencoolen Street | tel. 63 38 18 66 | www.strandhotel.com.sg | MRT CC 1, NS 24, NE 6 Dhoby Ghaut, then bus 64, 65*

YMCA INTERNATIONAL HOUSE ★
(130 B6) (*🕮 H3*)

You do not have to be a Christian, or young, or even male to be able to stay in one of these two guesthouses, but you do have to be quick. The very attractive price of the rooms means that they are in great demand – especially those in the centrally located *International House*. The surprisingly lavish – in this price category – amenities with swimming pool, squash courts, fitness centre, coffee shop and international direct-dial telephones in the simply furnished rooms can also be found in the more distant *YMCA Metropolitan* (128–129 C–D1) (*🕮 O*) *(92 rooms | 60 Stevens Road | tel. 68 39 83 33 | www.mymca.org.sg | MRT NS 22 Orchard, then bus 190). 106 rooms | 1 Orchard Road | tel. 63 36 60 00 | www.ymcaih.com.sg | MRT CC 1, NS 24, NE 6 Dhoby Ghaut*

Inexpensive but comfortable: YMCA International House

APARTMENTS, PRIVATE ROOMS & HOSTELS

Renting rooms in private homes is still not as widespread in Singapore as it is in many other of the world's metropolises. Here, this new branch is only developing slowly. This is because the rents paid for the old Chinese shophouses are so high – often more than 15,000 dollars a month – that it simply does not add up to offer only a few rooms to guests. However, you can try your luck on several Internet sites including z. B. *www.easyroommate.com.sg | www.ibilik.sg | www.roomorama.com/singapore*.

Hostels are an economical alternative in the city state. Among those providing beds and simple rooms are the very hospitable *Pillows & Toast (40 Mosque Street | tel. 62 20 46 53 www.pillowsntoast.com | MRT NE 4, DT 19 Chinatown)* in the heart of Chinatown. One alternative is Singapore's 'first indie boutique hostel": *Shophouse – The Social Hostel (48 Arab Street | tel. 62 98 87 21 | www.shophousehostel.com | MRT EW 12, DT 14 Bugis)* by the large mosque in the new in quarter Kampong Glam.

DISCOVERY TOURS

1 SINGAPORE AT A GLANCE

START: ① Botanic Gardens
END: ⑭ 1-Altitude

1 day
Actual walking time
2 hours

Distance:
21 km/13 mi (8.5 km/5.3 mi on foot)

COSTS: approx. 40 S$ without food and drink
WHAT TO PACK: Sunscreen and water, if you don't want to stop off specially too often; in the rainy season, an umbrella

IMPORTANT TIPS: For individual stages of the tour, take a taxi, rickshaw or the underground.

From tai chi under tropical trees to a nightcap in one of the most beautiful rooftop bars in south-east Asia – in the coming hours you'll get to know Singapore in all its variety. Naturally, this also includes the districts of Chinatown and Little India. But it's also worth exploring its colonial heritage and the famous Raffles Hotel.

 Photo: Cavenagh Bridge in front of the Esplanade Theatre and Suntec City

Cities have many faces. If you want to get behind the scenes to explore their unique charm and head off the beaten track or find your way to green oases, handpicked restaurants or the best local activities, then these tailored Discovery Tours are just the right thing. Choose the best route for the day and follow in the footsteps of the MARCO POLO authors – well-prepared to navigate your way to all the many highlights that await you along the tour.

07:30am The best way to work off the effects of your long flight is with some INSIDER TIP early-morning Chinese sport in the fresh air: in Singapore's old ❶ **Botanic Gardens → p. 57** there are a number of groups which offer free tai chi, gymnastics or fan dance. You can join in wearing your normal clothes. **The simplest way is to head for the large open space at the Visitor Centre (Cluny Park Gate),** where dozens of early-morning exercisers get together when it's not raining. After that you will have earned your breakfast against this green backdrop. The **Casa Verde**

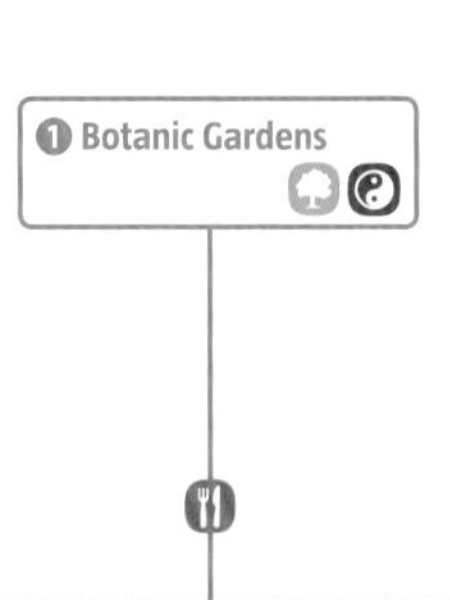

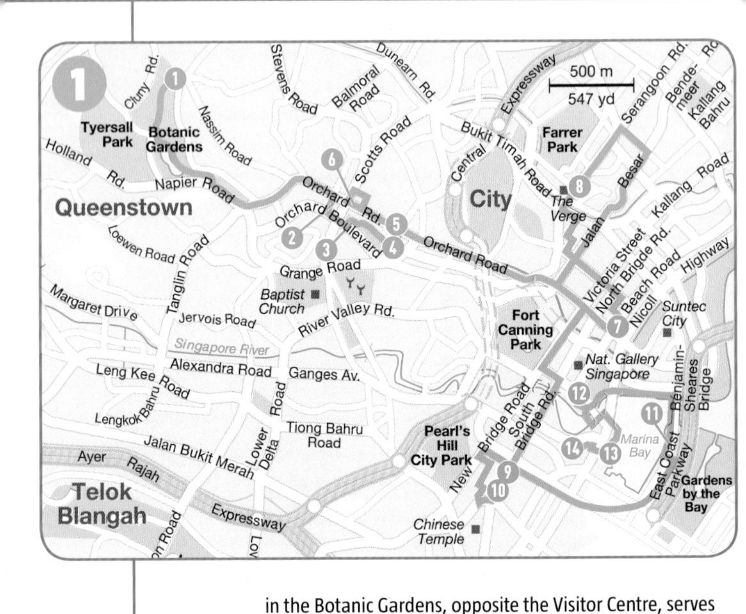

in the Botanic Gardens, opposite the Visitor Centre, serves baguettes as well as Asian rice dishes. Afterwards, take a walk through the garden underneath the magnificient tropical trees. The dazzling display of blossoms and their early-morning scent will get your day off to a good start. **Follow the signs to the Tanglin Gate. Cross the road and take the bus (7, 77, 106, 123, 174) in front of the Gleneagles Hospital as far as the Thai Embassy in the city centre. Cross Singapore's main thoroughfare, Orchard Road → p. 35, at the pedestrian crossing and keep to the left.** At the junction, enter the glass pyramid on ❷ **Wheelock Place**. The escalator takes you down to the second basement level – now you are standing in the heart of Singapore's shopping district, in the exclusive ❸ **ION Orchard** → **p. 75** centre which has over a hundred shops. Still underground, protected against the rain and the sun, stroll over to the traditional ❹ **Takashimaya** → **p. 76** department store which is the place to go for Asian brands. **After that, cross over the street from Takashimaya** and visit the attractive shopping centre ❺ **The Paragon** → **p. 36** as well as the traditional Singaporean department store ❻ **Tangs**.

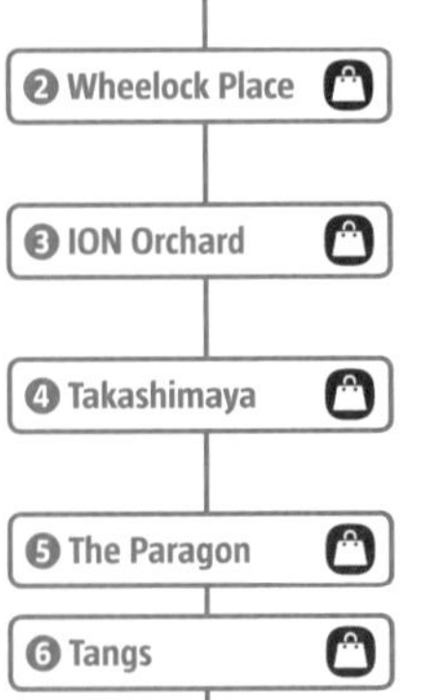

12:00pm **In front of the Marriott Hotel next door to Tangs take a taxi and drive up Orchard Road into the old Colonial Quarter** and on to your next destination, the

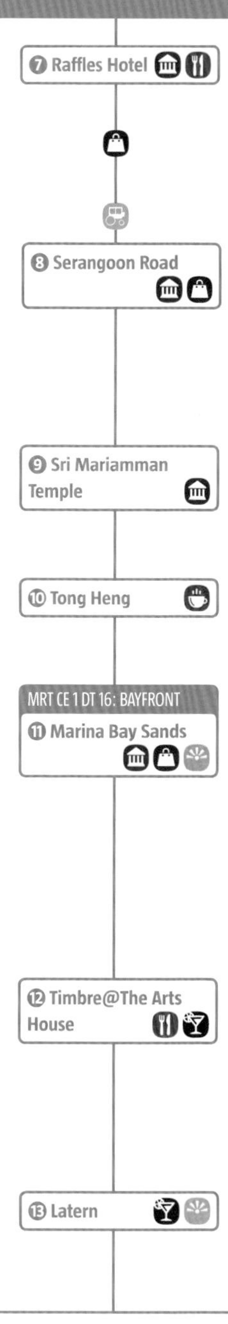

7 **Raffles Hotel** → p. 36, a gem from the colonial era. Brunch is served in the Billiard Room. The quality of the food is outstanding; some people come here especially for the INSIDER TIP desserts. The **souvenir shop** → p. 81 behind the restaurant is delightful, but expensive. **Outside Raffles, hire a rickshaw (they usually stand at the corner of Beach Road/Bras Basah Road) and have yourself chauffered along** 8 **Serangoon Road** → p. 27, the main street through Little India. From here, drift off into the side streets following the scent of jasmine and curry. **A taxi will bring you quickly back to** **Chinatown** → p. 46, where the city has its origins. Wander through the narrow streets, but don't trust the tailors who make tantalising offers of suits, but do peep into the cooking pots of the many street food vendors. Chinatown is where the the various cultures come together: at its heart is the Hindu 9 **Sri Mariamman Temple** → p. 48, where priests, worshippers and tourists celebrate a noisy get-together. If your legs are starting to ache, stop for a coffee break in one of Singapore's oldest bakeries: diagonally opposite the Sri Mariamman Temple is the traditional bakers's 10 **Tong Heng** *(285 South Bridge Road)*, famous for its warm egg tarts. If you are on a diet, plump for the **Tea Chapter** → p. 64, to witness a traditional Chinese tea ceremony. Then travel by underground railway from Chinatown station to Bayfront as far as 11 **Marina Bay Sands** → p. 42. Singapore's new landmark development includes the largest casino in the city and countless luxury boutiques. It is most famous, however, for its rooftop terrace high above the hotel. Some have dubbed it the 'ironing board', others say it resembles a boat. Nowhere, though, will you get a more beautiful view of the sunset.

07:00pm **Now stroll past the stages of the Esplanade → p. 40 along the romantic path beside the bay as far as** **The Arts House** → p. 31. Here, choose a table on the terrace of the 12 **Timbre@The Arts House** → p. 87 for a fabulous view across the brightly lit banking district. If you're not particularly hungry, go for the tapas; if you could do with something more substantial, there are noodles or fish. **After dinner, cross over Cavenagh Bridge with its splendid cast-iron framework and go through the underpass at the Fullerton Hotel to return to the bay.** To your right is the Fullerton Bay Hotel. The pretty rooftop terrace at the ★ 13 **Lantern** is the perfect place to chill out – and mark the start of the evening with a sensational view over Marina Bay. To round things off, head up high onto the

rooftop bar of the ⑭ **1-Altitude** → p. 84. Hot rhythms at the open-air disco and cool drinks in the night-time breeze – experience the tropics at their most beautiful.

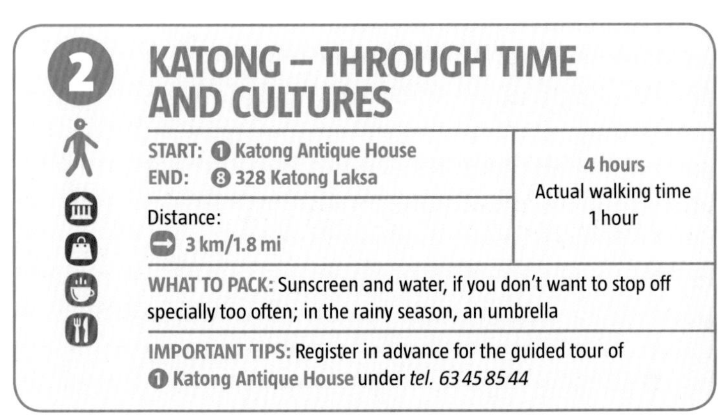

2 KATONG – THROUGH TIME AND CULTURES

START: ① Katong Antique House
END: ⑧ 328 Katong Laksa

4 hours
Actual walking time
1 hour

Distance:
3 km/1.8 mi

WHAT TO PACK: Sunscreen and water, if you don't want to stop off specially too often; in the rainy season, an umbrella

IMPORTANT TIPS: Register in advance for the guided tour of ① Katong Antique House under *tel. 63 45 85 44*

Walk for an afternoon in the footsteps of the early Singaporeans – Katong is the district of the Peranakan. This is the name of the ethnic group which developed out of the early Chinese, European and Malay settlers. They have left their mark on 'Little Singapore', as Katong is known – with their food, their architecture as well as their clothing.

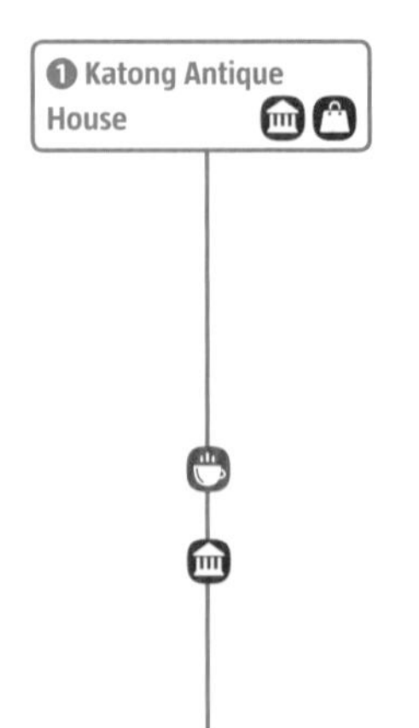

Stroll along both sides of East Coast Road – the main axis in Katong – for a close look at Singapore and its unique architecture. Do not expect to see anything spectacular, but you will gain an insight into everyday life. The walk begins at around 2pm at ① INSIDER TIP **Katong Antique House** *(208 East Coast Road | MRT NS 22 Orchard, then bus 14)*. You will discover a world all of its own behind this pale yellow house's modest wooden door: Peter Wee, whose father once owned a whole street of houses here, will lead you through the Museum of Peranakan Culture *(approx. 45 mins.)*. There is a small shop selling genuine, but expensive Peranakan antiques on the ground floor. **Turn left when you leave the small museum.** You will immediately come across the **Chin Mee Chin Confectionery** *(Closed Mon)*, one of Singapore's traditional bakeries. **Continue walking until you come to an narrow street which is worth taking a closer look at:** old, single-storey former officers' quarters still stand here. Now painted in bright colours, the small villas were built on pillars to protect them from flood waters. At the next set of traffic lights you come

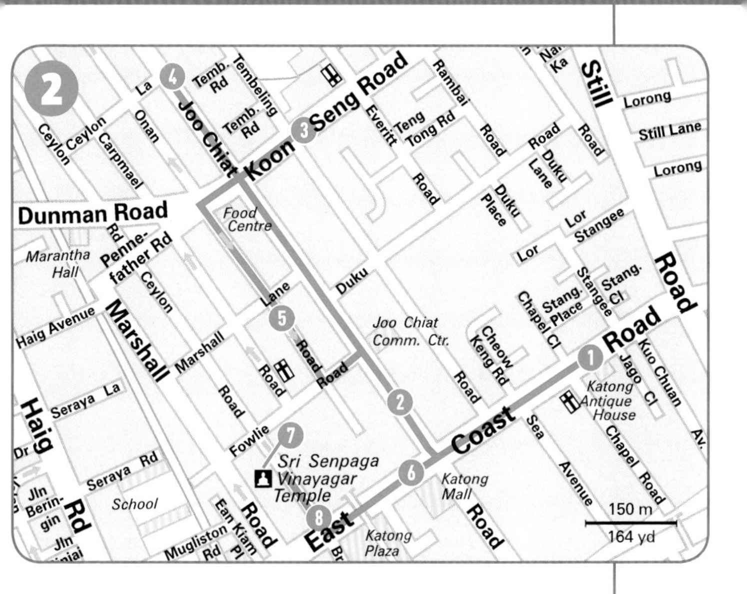

to Brotzeit, a pleasant restaurant catering mainly to European tastes. **Cross the road here and turn into ❷ Joo Chiat Road**. The sweetest temptation awaits you on the right-hand side on the corner: **Awfully Chocolate**. The shop is decorated completely in white and sells little else but all manner of dark chocolate – expensive, but good quality. Immediately after that you will get a whiff of the real Singapore: the bakers in **Puteri Mas** *(No. 475)* bake genuine durian cakes. It is forbidden to eat the 'stinking fruit' on buses and in the underground because of its pungent, cheesy smell, but it is considered a delicacy. Further along, on the left-hand side, the warm, filled dim sum dumplings on sale at **D'bun Freshly Handmade Bun Specialist** *(No.356)* are also delicious. **A good way further up the road on the left is the Ann Tin Tong Medical Hall** *(No. 320)*, a 70-year-old chemist's which employs a doctor and still mixes its teas and tinctures on the premises. **Just a few steps away on the right, you come to ❸ Koon Seng Road**. Its ensemble of houses is unique in Singapore. Their façades, decorated with stucco, combine Victorian and Chinese elements. The house fronts bear symbols of happiness and long life, such as bats, dragons, deer and dogs. They are made even more attractive by the application of old tiles which were imported at great cost from Europe. **Walk back a little way up Joo Chiat Road. A few hundred yards further on, you will dis-**

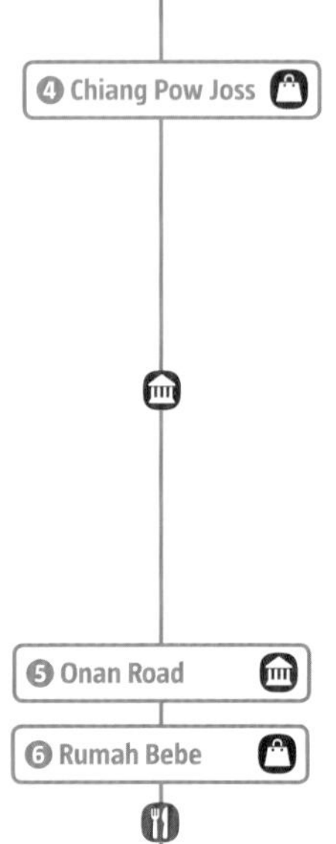

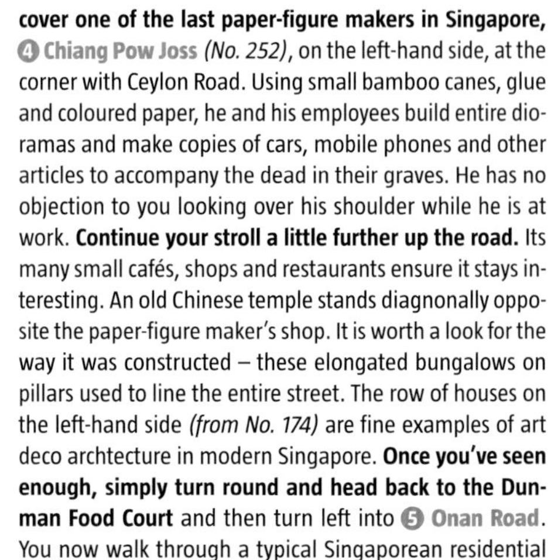

cover one of the last paper-figure makers in Singapore, ④ **Chiang Pow Joss** *(No. 252)*, on the left-hand side, at the corner with Ceylon Road. Using small bamboo canes, glue and coloured paper, he and his employees build entire dioramas and make copies of cars, mobile phones and other articles to accompany the dead in their graves. He has no objection to you looking over his shoulder while he is at work. **Continue your stroll a little further up the road.** Its many small cafés, shops and restaurants ensure it stays interesting. An old Chinese temple stands diagnonally opposite the paper-figure maker's shop. It is worth a look for the way it was constructed – these elongated bungalows on pillars used to line the entire street. The row of houses on the left-hand side *(from No. 174)* are fine examples of art deco archtecture in modern Singapore. **Once you've seen enough, simply turn round and head back to the Dunman Food Court** and then turn left into ⑤ **Onan Road**. You now walk through a typical Singaporean residential district with mango trees in the front gardens until you reach the main road again.

Victorian meets Chinese: architecture on Koon Seng Road

Turn left into Fowlie Road and then right onto Joo Chiat Road. From here you can get back onto East Coast Road again. Stay on the right until you reach ⑥ **Rumah Bebe** *(www.rumahbebe.com)*, the 'House of Bebe'. This is an excellent place to buy some beautiful souvenirs. The owner, Bebe Seet, is a real expert in the traditional art of embroidering shoes and clothes with pearls. She even gives 'beading' lessons in her house *(around 250 S$ including materials)*. **Rumah Kim Choo** and **Kim Choo's Kitchen** are right next door. Here, however, the glutamate which is otherwise used extensively as a flavour enhancer in Singapore is replaced with a home-made broth made with chicken bones, ginger and garlic – and the food tastes really good. Restaurateur Desmond Wong will be happy to answer any questions you still have on the fascinating Peranakan culture after your walk. **Turn right onto**

Ceylon Road and wind up your walk through the cultures with a dash of Hinduism. This is the location of the ❼ **Sri Senpaga Vinayagar Temple**, built by Indian Tamils in 1875 underneath a senpaga tree in honour of the elephant god. **Head back onto East Coast Road** and bring the evening to a traditional close: the hot noodle soup at the famous snack-bar ❽ **328 Katong Laksa** → p. 69 right on the corner is the best you'll find anywhere in the city.

❸ ROMANTIC SINGAPORE

START: ❶ Elgin Bridge
END: ❼ Makansutra Gluttons Bay

Distance: 2 km/1.2 mi

3.5 hours
Actual walking time 30 minutes

WHAT TO PACK: Water, if you don't want to stop off specially too often; in the rainy season, an umbrella

IMPORTANT TIPS: The ❹ pleasure cruisers leave every 15 minutes, daily between 9am and 10.30pm.

An Asian metropolis is seldom romantic, but usually colourful and full of hustle and bustle. Singapore's Colonial Quarter develops a very special charm after nightfall, (daily at around 7.30pm). Of course, you can also do the hour-and-a-half walk during the day, but it is especially captivating in the evening, when the old lanterns twinkle under the tropical trees.

The starting point of this walk is at ❶ **Elgin Bridge** *(MRT NE 5 Clarke Quay)*, close to Singapore's Parliament House, that connects South und North Bridge Roads. It was the first bridge in Singapore (1823) and is an important artery in the city since it acts as a link between Tua Po and Sio Po – the large and the small city, in the dialect of the Fujian Chinese. These indicate Singapore's administrative district and Chinatown, the commercial district on the other side of the river. **The Parliament is on your left-hand side as you stand on the left bank of the river looking towards the brightly illuminated skyscrapers of the financial institutions. To the side of the Parliament, go down the few steps to the river** and take a break on one of the many benches to admire the magnificent panorama. **Stroll a little further along the river bank as far as the floodlit** ❷ **statue of Singapore's founding father, Sir Thomas**

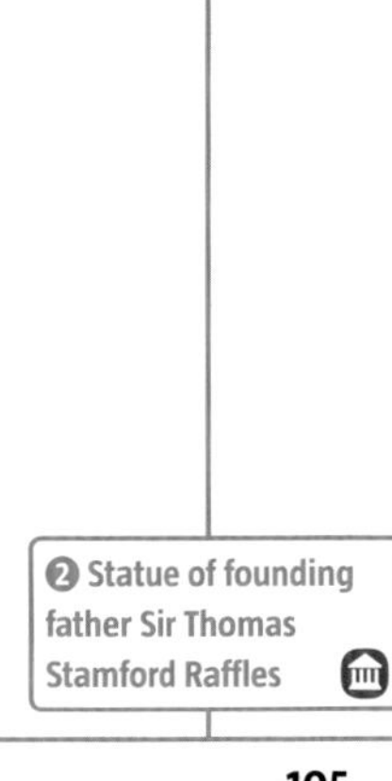

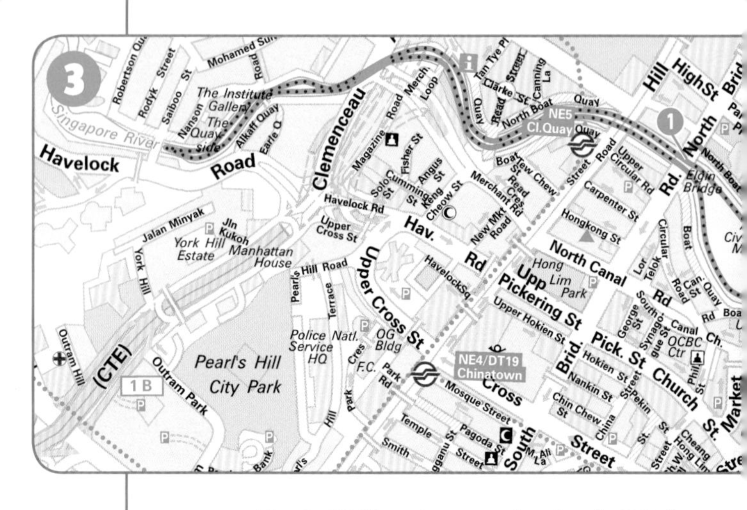

Stamford Raffles, who came ashore here in 1819. If you walk past 'stony' Raffles and beneath the overhanging branches and aerial roots of the tropical trees, you will soon reach the painstakingly renovated ❸ **Asian Civilisations Museum** → **p. 32**. On the steps you are greeted by silent witnesses to the past: sculptors Chern Lian Shan and Malcolm Kok have positioned life-size statues of the coolies and merchants who laid the foundations for Singapore's prosperity along the river many years ago. The Indian Chettiar, the money-lenders, negotiate with a female stockbroker who appears to have just come out of one of the bank towers on the opposite side of the river. The museum is well worth a visit and is open until 9pm on Fridays. **Afterwards, turn left and cross the bridge to the opposite bank of the river.** A number of ❹ **pleasure cruisers** *(24 S$)* are moored at the Fullerton Hotel. The 40-minute trip could hardly be more romantic. At the same time, you can find out a lot about the history of the old commercial docks. **Back on land, cross the historic, beautifully floodlit** ❺ **Cavenagh-Bridge** (1868) and return to the other side of the river. Singaporean couples like to be photographed under the trees to the left and right when they get married; the bank towers in the background are thought to auger prosperity. **Continue along the riverside path that now makes two slight curves before leading into a tunnel. The Queen Elizabeth Walk along Esplanade Park starts on the other side. If you walk further along the bay and then under the highway bridge, you finally arrive at the brightly**

❸ Asian Civilisations Museum

❹ Pleasure cruisers

❺ Cavenagh Bridge

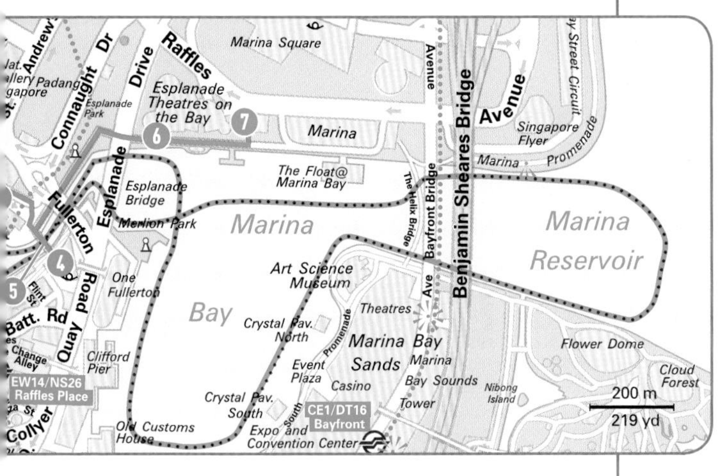

lit ❻ **Esplanade** → p. 40. **INSIDER TIP** Singaporean bands give free concerts on Friday, Saturday and Sunday evenings on the open-air stage by the water. On the right, behind the building, there is also an open-air *hawker centre*. In ❼ **Makansutra Gluttons Bay** → p. 66 the government has brought together the best hawker restaurants in Singapore. For just a few dollars, you can enjoy a delicous evening meal under the starry tropical skies.

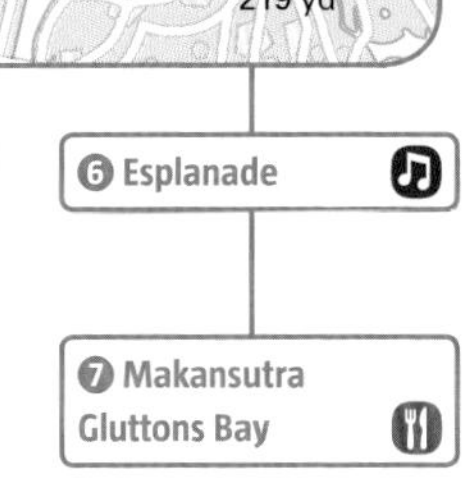

THE SOUTHERN RIDGES – CITY IN A GARDEN

START: ❶ Hort Park
END: ❽ Vivo City

Distance: 4.5 km/2.8 mi

Difficulty: easy

3 hours
Actual walking time 1.5 hours

WHAT TO PACK: Be sure to take water and sunscreen with you; in the rainy season, an umbrella.

IMPORTANT TIPS: It's a good idea to begin the walk early, before the sun gets too hot. Drink plenty of water and take lots of breaks on your way.

Singapore considered itself a garden city for many years. It now officially calls itself a 'City in a Garden'. In the course of this development, the individual hiking

paths were linked to form a circular route around the inner city – the ★ Southern Ridges. The path is extremely well thought-out and does not require any special preparations.

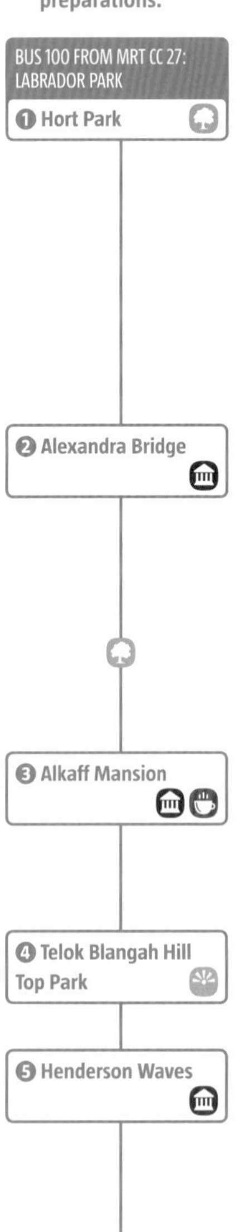

Take a taxi or bus so that you get to the car park of the ❶ Hort Park *(Alexandra Road)* **at around 9am**. The park itself is a large exhibition area where Singapore's garden specialists show what they are capable of. You will be enchanted by the articstically-designed gardens, fountains and examples of façade greening systems on display. It was here that experiments were carried out to ensure that the glass roof constructon of the enormous greenhouses in the Gardens by the Bay would let sufficient light but not too much direct sun into the cool glass houses. Singapore's new gallery district is developing in the former Gillman Barracks → p. 78 a little further along Alexandra Road towards the harbour. **However, you stay in the park and cross** the metal **❷ Alexandra Bridge** which curves elegantly in the form of a leaf above Alexandra Road. LED lights immerse the bridge in a sea of colours after night falls. **When you reach the end of the bridge, follow the steel construction, at the same height as the treetops. Continue up the secure metal steps for about 20 minutes and keep your eye on your surroundings.** You will discover birds and lizards and, if you look closely through the trees, whole herds of monkeys. But please don't feed them; they can become aggressive. **On your way up the mountain, you pass the ❸ Alkaff Mansion** *(10 Telok Blangah Green | alkaff.com.sg)*. The old colonial house from 1918, once owned by an Arab merchant, now houses an Italian restaurant *(Mon–Fri 11.30am–3pm, Mon–Sun 6pm–11pm | Expensive)*. Have a coffee to get your strength back. **If you continue along the path you will soon reach the highest point in the ❹ Telok Blangah Hill Top Park**. This is the perfect place to catch your breath and admire the panoramic view over Singapore through the dazzling bougainvillea bushes. **This is also where you set out for the ❺ Henderson Waves** – an amazing wooden bridge that arches 36 m/118 ft above Henderson Road and links the Telok Blangah Hill Park with Mount Faber. The American architect Daniel Libeskind designed the towers shining in the sun on the right which appear to rise out of the jungle in front of the harbour. Children love the alcoves formed by the curves of the wooden bridge which was built using yellow south-east Asian bakau wood.

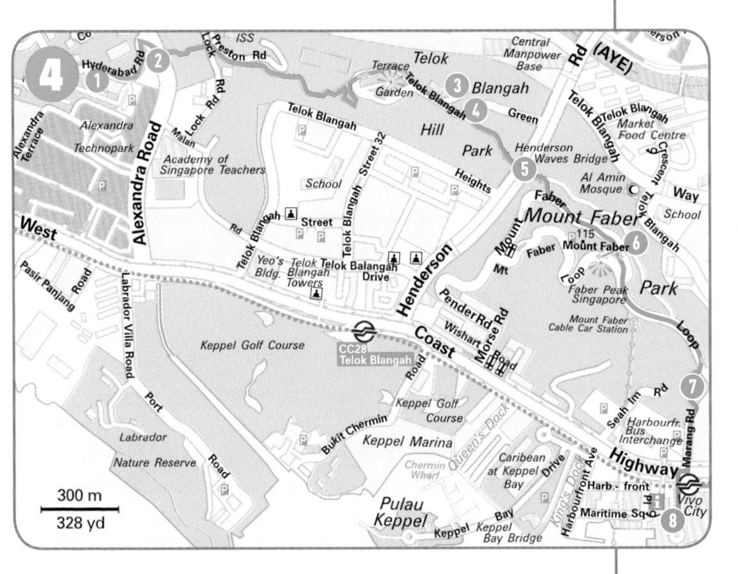

You have now reached ⑥ **Mount Faber** → p. 54. If the weather is fine, you'll be able to see as far as Sumatra. The jungle here covers an area of more than 56 ha/138 ac. The **Faber Peak Singapore** → p. 54 with its restaurants and bars is located at the very top of Singapore's 'own' mountain. From here, there is a stunning view of Sentosa, the important harbour and the busy Straits of Malacca, the main shipping route to China and Japan. The harbour is responsible for seven percent of Singapore's economic output. You can also take the cable car over to Sentosa from here, but save this for another day, as you still have the interesting descent ahead of you: the ⑦ **Marang Trail** is the least developed section of the path for tourists. Sometimes, after a tropical storm, the odd tree can lie across the steps. **Follow the signposts along the road, over the crest of the mountain to Car Park B and then to the right, behind the building and down into the valley.** If you are lucky, you might be here when the saga trees are wearing their dazzling red pearls – they are often used to make jewellery. **Now the path goes steeply down towards the harbour.** The jungle only opens up to give a view of it at the very last moment: you realise you are back in civilization when you turn the last bend and suddenly catch sight of the glaringly white Vivo City shopping centre, plus the underground station and six-lane harbour road. **The**

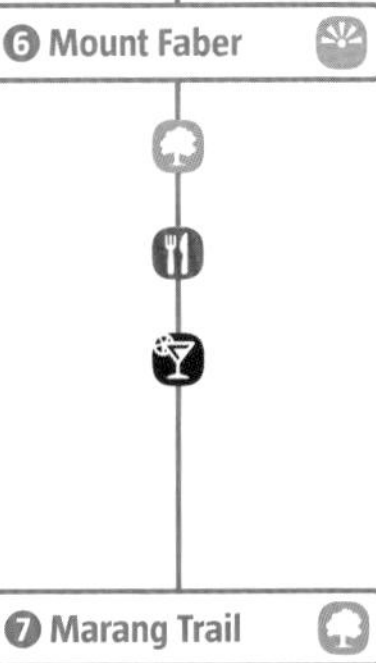

Back in the cool of civilization: a refreshing end to your walk at Vivo City

8 Vivo City

path downhill takes around a quarter of an hour. Cross the road and walk through the attractive shopping centre **8 Vivo City** → p. 57 – take care not to catch cold, though, if you're still sweating from your walk; the air-conditioning is pretty powerful. There are dozens of cafés along the waterside of Vivo City in which you can relax and round off your ramble through the 'city garden' with a good cup of coffee or an ice cream.

5 TIONG BAHRU – DIP INTO THE MELTING POT

START: 1 Tiong Bahru underground station
END: 9 Tiong Bahru market

Distance:
2 km/1.2 mi

4 hours
Actual walking time 30 minutes

WHAT TO PACK: Water and sunscreen; in the rainy season, an umbrella.

IMPORTANT TIPS: Most cafés and shops are closed on Mondays.

Tiong Bahru is Singapore at its most attractive – as a melting pot. In no other quarter is the mixture of young and old, Singaporean and foreigner, in-crowd and social-housing resident as noticeable as here. The magnificent architecture is

unique, some is reminiscent of the Paris or Berlin of the early 1920s, but with an Asian touch. We recommend you visit Tiong Bahru on a Saturday morning and mingle with the crowds.

Take the underground railway to ❶ Tiong Bahru station. When you leave the station by the Tiong Bahru Plaza exit, keep to the left. Cross Tiong Bahru Road at the pedestrian crossing and go on down to the left. Then turn right into Kim Pong Road. All of a sudden, the view around you changes completely: gone are the high-rise complexes; before you lies an ensemble of delightful white art-deco buildings. They were built between the late 1930s and the 1950s, originally as social housing. Because they appeared so modern in the eyes of the Singaporeans and due to their wing-like form, they were nicknamed the 'Aero-Flats'. **At the end of the road you come to two fine restaurants on Moh Guan Terrace**; or are there actually three? The rear section of the eatery on the left-hand side, the traditional Chinese noodle restaurant **Hua Bee** *(daily 7am–2.30am)*, becomes a modern, Japanese restaurant *(daily noon–3pm and 6pm–midnight)* – in this way the leaseholders reduce the high rents. The noodles are just as good as the Japanese dishes. On the right-hand side is the Australian-style Flock Café *(daily 8am–6pm)*. Walk past the café and take a stroll down ❷ **Yong Siak Street**. This is where young entrepreneurs have opened shops and restaurants in old houses. To the left is the PoTeaTo Bistro Café, a few yards further along, the **40 Hands** → p. 63. Long-standing residents love it here in particular because of the good coffee. Cross over to the other side of the street and browse the shelves at **Books Actually** → p. 74. It's a combination of literary book shop, local meeting place and antique dealer's. Take a look at the choice of scene and city magazines. A little further on, **Woods in the Books** *(Tue–Sat 11am–8pm, Sun 11am–6pm)* has a large selection of English-language books for children. It's now time, though, for a coffee: wander on down to the INSIDER TIP **Plain Vanilla Bakery** *(Tue–Fri 11am–8pm, Sat 9am–8pm, Sun 9am–6pm)*. The wonderful smell is enough to enchant anyone; but you can also take a peek over the bakers' shoulders as they work. If you wish, you can hire one of the turquoise-coloured bicycles (10 S$/hr) for the rest of the tour.

Keep to the left on ❸ Chay Yan Street. The overhanging roofs of the traditional houses provide welcome shade and

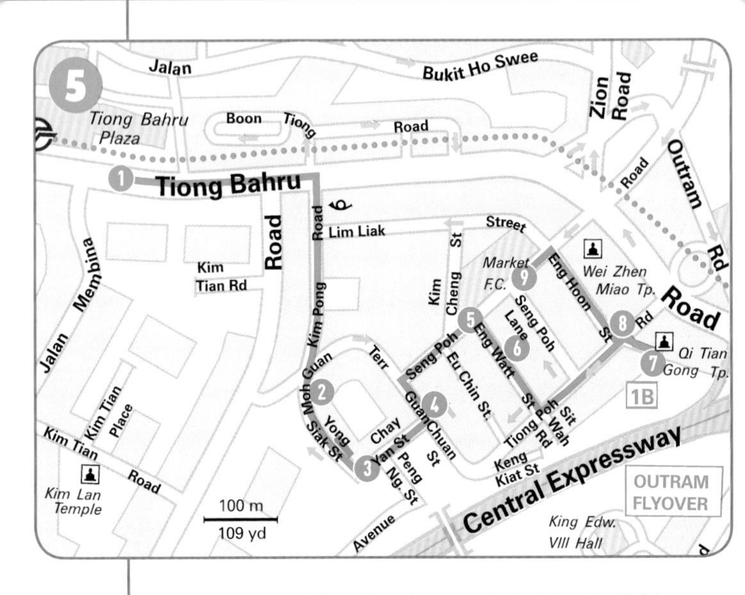

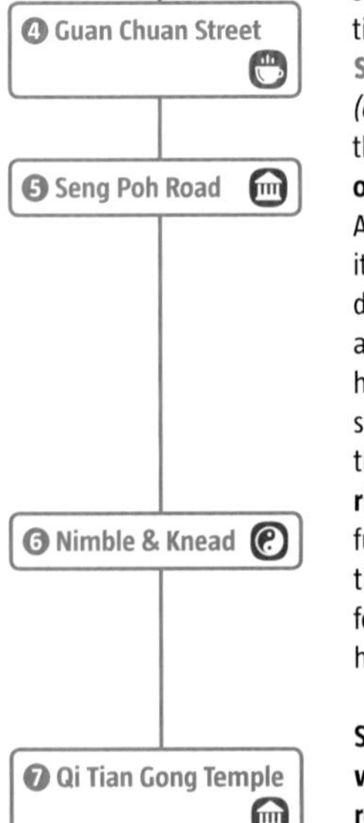

protect from the rain. Take a look at No. 26 which houses the **White Space Art Asia** *(Tue–Sun 11am–8pm)* gallery. Everywhere in this quarter you will find informative, large signs in English depicting its history; it's worth taking the time to read them. **Now turn left into 4 Guan Chuan Street**, where there's a branch of the well-known **PS. Café** *(daily 11am–11pm)*. If you like Australian cakes and burgers, this is the place to indulge. **A detour to the right takes you onto the district's main thorouhfare, 5 Seng Poh Road**. Although Tiong Bahru is now very popular with foreigners, its Chinese roots cannot be overlooked: the houses are decorated with lanterns at Chinese New Year. Again and again you will discover tiny altars set into the walls of the houses. And look out for the staircases, balconies and the shapes of the doors and windows – you won't find anything comparable in the rest of today's Singapore. **Turn right into Eng Watt Street.** If you fancy a massage, look no further. **6 Nimble & Knead** promises to give your muscles the once-over until they are as 'soft as dough'. The price for a one-hour foot massage starts at 42 S$. Often half an hour is enough.

Suitably invigorated, continue left onto Tiong Poh Road, which you follow downhill. Diagonally opposite at the road junction stands the 7 Qi Tian Gong Temple, the first in Singapore to be dedicated to the monkey god. He is said to bring happiness, prosperity and also ingenuity. Here, at the latest, you will notice that this is no Western metropolis, but a thoroughly Asian city. **Now turn into ⑧ Eng Hoon Street** behind you. On the right-hand side you will soon come across the well-known **Tiong Bahru Bakery** – founded by a Frenchman, it is expensive, but fantastic. It's worth popping into **Nana & Bird** *(Tue–Fri noon–7pm, Sat/Sun 11am–7pm)* opposite. The boutique, which has two branches in the district, sells clothes and accessories by a number of Singaporean designers. **You reach the heart of the district at the far end of the street:** the **⑨ Tiong Bahru Market**. The two-storey building has hardly changed in the last 50 years, despite being renovated. Here, you will still see older generations, the 'uncles' and 'aunties', doing their shopping. Downstairs, vegetables and meat, household goods and plastic flowers are on sale; upstairs is one of the best *hawker centres* in the city. More than 20 of the local snack bars are so popular that they have been successfully doing business for over 30 years. Stand No. 82, for example, offers traditional boneless chicken and rice. Two stands further along, at Nr. 30, there are Wanton noodles. The best idea is just to wander along from one stand to the next and take a peek into the cooking pots. As a rule of thumb: the longer the queue at the stand, the better the food.

⑧ Eng Hoon Street

⑨ Tiong Bahru Market

Culmination of the tour: lunch at one of the best *hawkers* in town, Tiong Bahru Market

TRAVEL WITH KIDS

Singapore is fond of children. People in the street will smile at your offspring. The two biggest attractions are still, of course, the *Zoo* (p. 60) and the *Resort World Sentosa* (p. 54). There are plenty of tips for your trip with children in *www.singaporeforkids.com*; adventures in the city are listed under *www.nparks.gov.sg/activities*.

AND IF IT RAINS

'Trampoline till you drop': *Amped* has large halls full of them, surrounded by thick cushions. Fun for young and old all over the city, e. g. *Mon 10am–7pm, Tue 3pm–10pm, Wed–Fri 10am–10pm, Sat 9am–10pm, Sun 9am–9pm | 12–18 S$, depending on the day | 46 Kim Yam Road | MRT NE 5 Clarke Quay*.

Or visit the *Singapore Discovery Centre* (0) (b4) *(Tue–Sun 9am–6pm | admission adults 10, children 6 S$ | 510 Upper Jurong Road | www.sdc.com.sg | bus 193, 182 from MRT EW 27 Boon Lay)*, which introduces them to all kinds of technology. The ★ *Singapore Science Centre* (0) (b4) *(daily 10am–6pm | admission adults 12, children 8 S$ | 15 Science Centre Road | www.science.edu.sg | bus 335 or 66 from MRT EW 24, NS 1 Jurong East)* is geared to the scientists of the future. If you need to cool down afterwards, head for the artificial ski slope at ● *Snow City* (skis for hire). The Imax cinema next door shows entertaining educational films.

The *Civil Defence Heritage Centre* (136 B1) (J4) *(Tue–Sun 10am–5pm | free admission | Central Fire Station | 62 Hill Street | www.scdf.gov.sg | MRT EW 13, NS 25 City Hall, NE 5 Clarke Quay, then bus 190)* sounds a bit war-like but it's here that the kids can become firefighters *(Sat 9am–11am)*.

PLAYGROUNDS

Children can have fun and learn a lot about nature in the ★ ● *Jacob Ballas Children's Garden* (128 A–B1) (0) *(daily 8am–7pm | Botanic Gardens | Cluny Road entrance | www.sbg.org.sg | MRT CC 19, DT 9 Botanic Gardens)* in the old Botanic Gardens. The youngsters can romp around in the fountains in the outdoor water-playground (138 C2) (D8) *(daily 10am–10pm | Telok Blangah Road/Sentosa Gateway | www.vivocity.com.sg | MRT NE 1, CC 29 S Habourfront)* in the courtyard on

That Jungle feeling! Anybody who thinks that Singapore is not a good place for children is keeping them from some fantastic experiences

the second floor of *Vivo City*. There are other INSIDER TIP large pools of water one floor higher up on the roof. There is even a covered playground for small children in the centre of the shopping centre *The Paragon* (129 F4–5) (*G2*) (*daily 10am–10pm | 290 Orchard Road | www.paragon.com.sg | MRT NS 22 Orchard Road*) on Level 5. The *Hip Kids Club* (*daily 10am–10pm | 583 Orchard Road | Level 2 | www.forumtheshoppingmall.com.sg | MRT NS 22 Orchard*) at the *Forum The Shopping Mall* (129 D4) (*E1*) offers a large, supervised play area for an annual fee of 15 S$.

PURE NATURE

The *HSBC* INSIDER TIP *Tree Top Walk* in the *MacRitchie Reserve* (0) (*c4*) (*Tue–Fri 9am–5pm, Sat/Sun 8.30am–5pm | free admission | Upper Thomson Road | Höhe Venus Drive | www.nparks.gov.sg | bus 132 from Orchard Road*) runs over a 250-m (273-yd)-long suspension bridge in the treetops. You will probably see lots of monkeys – but remember that it is strictly forbidden to feed them.

At the southern entrance you can hire a kayak at the *Paddle Lodge* (*daily 9am–noon, 2pm–6pm | kayak 15 S$/hr | Lornie Road | tel. 62 62 58 00 57 | www.scf.org.sg | MRT NS 22 Orchard, then bus 167 from Orchard Boulevard*) for a paddle across the lake under jungle vegetation.

TOURS ● (137 D1) (*K3*)

Tours of the city with the *Singapore Duck* are really exciting. The old, brightly coloured, US-Army amphibious vehicles drive through the Colonial Quarter and then straight into the water; *depart on the hour 10am–6pm | adults 37, children from 3–12 27 S$ | 3 Temasek Blvd. | #01–330 | Suntec City | tel. 63 38 68 77 | www.ducktours.com.sg | MRT CC 3 Esplanade*

FESTIVALS & EVENTS

Buddhists, Christians, Hindus and Muslims – each religious group is granted two public holidays in Singapore. The major holidays of the religious and ethnic groups are also days off for everyone else, although the shops open their doors.

EVENTS

JANUARY/FEBRUARY

★ ***Chinese New Year:*** The excitement can be felt throughout the city days before: houses and streets are decorated in red and gold, and the shopping centres vie for business. Groups of drummers appear, and lion and dragon dancers make their way through the streets. A highlight is the spectacular ***firework display*** at the harbour.

FEBRUARY

INSIDER TIP ***Thaipusam*** the celebrations honouring the Hindu god Muruga are really dramatic: the faithful bore the ends of the wires of the 'Kavadi', cages decorated with peacock feathers, into their skin: the metal constructions are then carried in processions through the streets. Some men walk the three kilometres from the Sri Srinivasa Perumal to the Sri Thendayuthapani temple wearing shoes of nails.

Chingay Parade: Carnival in Singapore! Dozens of groups and acrobats make their way across the arena at the Formula 1 track and guarantee that the spectators have a good time. Noisy, colourful and with many circus-like interludes.

MARCH/APRIL

INSIDER TIP ***Ching Ming Festival***: A Chinese mixture of All Saints' Day and Easter. Mercedes Benz cars, Rolex watches and computers are set ablaze at the cemeteries – but, these treasures are only made of paper. The smoke transports them to the other world where they make the life of the departed more luxurious.

MAY/JUNE

INSIDER TIP ***Great Singapore Sale***: Of course, you can shop twelve months a year, but it is even more fun during the Great Sale – and you can save money.

JUNE

Dragon Boat Festival: This festival was initiated in memory of the Chinese schol-

Singapore's colourful calendar of festivities is characterised by tolerance: there are two public holidays for each religion

ar Qu Yuan who drowned himself 2400 years ago because he was so distressed about the corruption in the country – today it is a spectacle on Marina Bay.

AUGUST

Hungry Spirits Festival: Small altars are set up all over town where offerings of fruit are made to the dead. The main centre is Chinatown.

SEPTEMBER/OCTOBER

Thimithi: Believers walk over glowing coals in honour of the goddess Draupathi in the Sri Mariamman Temple.

Formula 1 night-time race

OCTOBER/NOVEMBER

Deepavali: Little India is even more dazzling during the Hindu Festival of Lights. Visitors delight in the food, aromas, dances and colourful clothing of the Indians.

PUBLIC HOLIDAYS

1 Jan	New Year's Day
late Jan/ early Feb	Chinese New Year
March/ April	Good Friday
1 May	Labour Day
late May/ early June	Vesak Day
late June 2017, mid-June 2018, early June 2019	*Hari Raya Puasa*
9 Aug	National Holiday
early Sept 2017, late Aug 2018 mid-Aug 2019	*Hari Raya Haji*
mid-Oct/ early Nov	*Deepavali*
25 Dec	Christmas

LINKS, BLOGS, APPS & MORE

www.timeoutsingapore.com The best website to find out about what is happening in Singapore; put together by the journalists of the city magazine of the same name

www.mrbrown.com A dash of satire about the 'fine city' for those in the know, written in a way that you can still laugh about it in Singapore

www.hungrygowhere.com/singapore For the hungry – the site Singaporeans consult for restaurant tips

www.airconditionednation.com The excellent collection of essays *Singapore: Air-Conditioned Nation* by the journalist Cherian George explains how politics and society function in Singapore

awards.nuffnang.com The best blogs about the region arranged by categories including fashion, lifestyle, influence, originality – and food of course

www.ladyironchef.com The witty restaurant reviews make this one of the top ten food blogs

ieatishootipost.sg This site provides a good overview of Singapore's food scene

localadventures.blogspot.com Locals reveal secrets about Singapore's nature in this blog. You will find information on hiking paths and rare animals

singart.com Singapore has developed into an art and culture hotspot – this website helps you to discover it

singaporerebel.blogspot.com Political and socio-critical blogs like this one are usually produced abroad, many of them by disgruntled Singaporeans

Regardless of whether you are still preparing your trip or already in Singapore: these addresses will provide you with more information, videos and networks to make your holiday even more enjoyable

www.sylistic.com/travel/category/singapore-2/ The newest Singapore travel forum has information on inexpensive accommodation offers

wiki.couchsurfing.org/en/Singapore The 'couch-surfing' network links travellers with people in other countries and cities; in this case, with Singapore

www.sgtravelcafe.com Network where Singaporeans exchange views – if you enter the word 'Singapore', you will get the best tips for their hometown

www.lonelyplanet.com/thorntree/forums/asia-south-east-asia-islands-peninsula/singapore The Thorntree Community exchanges experiences and useful tips about Singapore: where you can find really inexpensive accommodation and which Chinese restaurant you should avoid at all cost

VIDEOS & MUSIC

www.youtube.com/watch?v=oYoAC3cLOgI&feature=related This deals exclusively – and humorously – with Singapore's favourite food: Pepper Crab

www.youtube.com/watch?v=0J1Ya5AwzGc&feature=related Background information and pictures of the construction of the Marina Bay Sands complex

www.youtube.com/watch?v=PVP1GdvD2L4 Although not bang up to date, this introduction to the city from Discovery Channel, including historical pictures, is extremely informative

APPS

iChangi The app for flights to and from Singapore's Changi Airport

gothere.sg Lost your bearings? This app helps you find your way round the city

grabtaxi and easytaxi Use these two apps to call a taxi (almost) anytime, anywhere in Singapore

TRAVEL TIPS

ARRIVAL

Most visitors land at Changi Airport (0) (e3–4). There are MRT stations directly under Terminals 2 and 3. The trains leave for the inner city every twelve minutes between 5.30am and 11.18 pm (Orchard by MRT NS 22); the trip costs 2.30 S$. The last MRT from the inner city leaves the Orchard Road Station at 11.25pm. The air-conditioned buses of line 36 also leave from the basement every ten minutes for the Orchard Road terminus. The fare is 2 S$. You must have the exact amount. There are also taxis (transfer time around 20 min, approx. 40 S$), maxi-cabs (for 7 persons from 40 S$), Mercedes limousines (from 45 S$) and hotel buses.

Cruise ships and the ferries to Batam dock at the Cruise Centre *(www.singaporecruise.com.sg)* near HarbourFront Centre (128 C2) *(B8)*. The MRT NE departs from there for Orchard Road (CC 1, NS 24, NE 6 Dhoby Ghaut). The ferries to the Southern Islands steam out of Marina South Pier *(MRT NS 28 Marina Pier* / www.islandcruise.com.sg). Ferries to Bintan depart from the Tanah Merah Ferry Terminal (0) *(e4)* (ideally by taxi). Good information on the islands and other excursions under: *www.wildsingapore.com* and *www.nparks.gov.sg.*

Express buses from Kuala Lumpur (min. 5 hours) arrive at Lavender Street Bus Station (131 E–F 2–3) *(L1)* *(MRT EW11 Lavender)* or at the Golden Mile Komplex (131 F5) *(L2)* *(MRT C5 Nicoll Highway)*.

RESPONSIBLE TRAVEL

It doesn't take a lot to be environmentally friendly whilst travelling. Don't just think about your carbon footprint whilst flying to and from your holiday destination but also about how you can protect nature and culture abroad. As a tourist it is especially important to respect nature, look out for local products, cycle instead of driving, save water and much more. If you would like to find out more about eco-tourism please visit: *www.ecotourism.org*

BANKS & CURRENCY EXCHANGE

The best exchange rates are offered by the offices with the 'Authorized Money Changer' signs in many shopping centres and streets. Avoid changing money in hotels – it can be very expensive. Some banks charge high fees for cashing traveller's cheques. However, the branches of the OCBC Bank exchange free of charge. The rates for exchanging money in Europe before you leave are unfavourable.

Banks in Singapore are usually open Mon–Fri 9.30am–3 or 4pm, Sat 9.30–11am. Several branches of the DBS Bank are open until 3pm on Saturdays. As anywhere in the world, the simplest way to get money are cash dispensers. Many of them accept Visa, American Express and MasterCard credit cards as do most of the larger shops.

From arrival to weather

Holiday from start to finish: the most important addresses and information for your Singapore trip

CLIMATE, WHEN TO GO

There are two seasons in Singapore but it is always very humid: the dry period (March–Oct) with high temperatures of around 33°C (92°F) and the rainy season (Nov–Feb) when the temperature can fall to 23°C (73°F).

CLOTHING

You should wear loose cotton clothes or other apparel suitable for hot weather. Do not forget an umbrella if you go for a long walk (tropical downpours!). You have to remove your shoes before entering Hindu temples and Muslim mosques.

CONSULATES & EMBASSIES

BRITISH HIGH COMMISSION
(120 B4) (*B2*) *100 Tanglin Road | Singapore 247919 | tel. +65 64 24 42 00 | ukinsingapore.fco.gov.uk*

CANADIAN HIGH COMMISSION
(122 C3) (*G5*) *One George Street, #11-01 | Singapore 049145 | tel. +65 68 54 59 00 | www.canada.gc.ca*

U.S. EMBASSY
(120 B4) (*B2*) *27 Napier Road | Singapore 258508 | tel. +65 64 76 91 00 | singapore.usembassy.gov*

CUSTOMS

You can import 1L of alcohol and a small amount of perfume for your personal use tax-free – but no cigarettes! It is forbidden to bring pornographic material and any kind of drugs into the country. *Customs information: (tel. 65 42 70 58 | tel. 63 55 20 00 | www.customs.gov.sg).*

BUDGETING

Coffee	£0.50–£2.80/ $0.80–$4.40 *for a cup of coffee*
Snack	£2–£3/ $3.30–$4.80 *for a serving of chicken rice in a food court*
Beer	£5–£10/ $7.80–$15.50 *for a glass of beer*
Boat trip	£7.30–£15/ $12–$24 *for a trip to the Southern Islands*
Souvenirs	£5–£6/ $7–$8 *for three table mats made of Chinese fabric*
Clothes	£2.50–£11/ $4–$17.50 *for a simple t-shirt*

The following goods can be exported duty-free when you leave Singapore: 200 cigarettes or 50 cigars or 250 g tobacco, 1 L of spirits or 4L wine, 250 g coffee and other good up to a value of £340/430 Euro.
Travellers to the US who are residents of the country do not have to pay duty on articles purchased overseas up to the

value of $800, but there are limits on the amount of alcoholic beverages and tobacco products. For the regulations for international travel for US residents please see *www.cbp.gov*.

ELECTRICITY

Mains voltage 220–240 volt, 50 hertz. Singapore has the same three-point plugs used in England. British plugs work in most hotels; three-point plugs are usual elsewhere (adapters from the hotel reception and in many shops).

EMERGENCY SERVICES

Police *(tel. 999)*, Ambulance & Fire Brigade *(tel. 995*
24-hour emergency service in hospitals: *Gleneagles Hospital (tel. 64737222)*; *Mount Elizabeth Hospital (tel. 67372666)* both are centrally located and recommendable

HEALTH

Vaccinations are not prescribed and are also not necessary unless you arrive from a yellow fever or cholera region. There is no danger of malaria in Singapore but dengue fever exists. It is completely safe to drink tap water. If you should need a doctor, ask your hotel.

IMMIGRATION

A visa is not required but a passport valid for more than six months is necessary. Your passport will be stamped permitting you to stay for up to 30 days *(extensions from the Immigration Department | tel. 63916100)*. A two-page *Landing Card* has to be completed before passport control; keep the copy until your departure.

INFORMATION BEFORE THE TRIP

SINGAPORE TOURISM BOARD

– *1–3 Strand Grand Buildings (c/o Singapore Centre) | London WC2N 5HR | tel. +44 (0)20 74 84 27 10 | stb_london@stb.gov.sg*
– *1156 Avenue of the Americas | Suite 702 | New York, NY 10036 | tel. +1 212 302 48 61 | newyork@stb.gov.sg*

INFORMATION IN SINGAPORE

SINGAPORE TOURISM BOARD (STB) VISITOR INFORMATION CENTRES

The centres are excellently equipped and it is especially worth visiting the one on Orchard Road.

– *Orchard Gateway* (130 A5) *(⊞ G2) (216 Orchard Road)*

ADDRESSES IN SINGAPORE

It takes some getting used to the way addresses are given in Singapore: in large buildings, the floor and room number are given. For example, British Airways' address is shown as 15 Cairnhill Road, #06–05 Cairnhill Place. This means that you will find the office at 15 Cairnhill Road on the sixth floor. The shops and offices on the individual floors also have house numbers – British Airways has got the number 5.

– *Chinatown Visitor Centre* (135 F4) (H5) *(2 Banda Street)*
Hotline: *tel. (free) 180 07 36 20 00*
Get basic information from the website of the Singapore Tourism Board *www.stb.com.sg* and at *www.yoursingapore.com*.

INTERNET & WI-FI

As almost everywhere else in the world, it makes sense here in Singapore to buy a SIM card for your mobile phone. The three telephone companies, Singapore Telecom (Singtel), Starhub and M1, offer a variety of prepaid cards. They have their own counters at the airport; in town, most money changers and 7 Eleven shops sell cards. All you need is your passport.
A local telephone number will allow you to log into the *wireless@SG* hotspots around the city.

PHONES & MOBILE PHONES

International phone calls can be made wherever you see the 'IDD' symbol. You can buy phonecards in telecom shops, post offices, 7-eleven shops and exchange offices (3–50 S$). There are credit-card phones at the airport, in post offices and telecom shops. You can make local calls free of charge from the airport. Dialling code for Singapore: *+65*; dialling code to the UK *+44*, US/Canada *+1*.

POST

The main post offices are *Tanglin Post Office* (128 C4) (D2) *(Mon–Fri 8.30am–5pm, Sat to 1pm | 56 Tanglin Road | opposite Tanglin Mall)* and *Orchard Post* (129 E4) (F2) *(Mon–Sun 11am–7pm | 2 Orchard Turn | #B2–62 | Ion Orchard)*. Your hotel reception will help you send letters abroad. *Singapore Post (www.singpost.com)* makes it possible for you to really surprise your friends and family at home: you can have INSIDER TIP your own photograph printed on a stamp in Singapore and then use it for your holiday post. The 'MyStamp' service is only available at *the post office at 1 Killiney Road (MRT NS 23 Somerset)* (130 A5) (G2). Bring your chosen motif with you on a USB stick.

CURRENCY CONVERTER

£	SGD	SGD	£
1	1.70	1	0.59
3	5.10	3	1.77
5	8.50	5	2.95
13	22.10	13	7.65
40	68	40	23.60
75	127.40	75	44.20
120	204	120	70.70
250	425	250	147.20
500	850	500	295

$	SGD	SGD	$
1	1.40	1	0.73
3	4.5	3	2.15
5	7.00	5	3.58
13	18.14	13	9.32
40	55.82	40	28.66
75	104.65	75	55.75
120	167.45	120	86
250	358.83	250	179.17
500	697.60	500	358,34

For current exchange rates see www.xe.com

PUBLIC TRANSPORT

Singapore's underground is air-conditioned and excellently organised. Mobile telephones even work in the tunnels.

There are currently five lines: the North East Line (NE), the East West Line (EW), the North South Line (NS), the Circle Line (CC) as well as the Downtown Line (DT). Construction of the sixth line, the Thomson East Coast Line (TEL), will continue until 2019. MRT fares range from 1 S$ to 2.40 S$, and the trains run in the municipal area from 5.30am to 0.30am.

Buses depart every six to thirty minutes from 5.15am to midnight. The fares range from 1 S$ to 2.60 S$ depending on the distance travelled. You can pay the driver in the bus – but be sure to have the exact amount.

The *EZ-link Card*, or *Easy Card (www.ezlink.com.sg)* for short, is a rechargable ticket for buses and MRT and costs 15 or 20 S$. This includes a non-refundable, one-off purchase fee of 5 S$. This card considerably reduces fares.

The *Singapore Tourist Pass* is a special EZ-link Card which is valid for one, two or three days for 20, 26 and 30 S$ and entitles the holder to unlimited travel in the corresponding period. The 10-S$ deposit is refunded when you return the card. Visitors can buy the cards and the useful *Transit Link Guide* (5.90 S$) at the main MRT stations such as NS 22 Orchard Road. Additional information under *www.smsrt.com.sg* and *www.sbstransit.com.sg*.

There are also many different passes with various combinations of public transport and admission to major attractions. One example is the *Go Singapore Pass (www.gosingaporepass.com.sg)*, a combination of the EZ-link

WEATHER IN SINGAPORE

	Jan	Feb	March	April	May	June	July	Aug	Sept	Oct	Nov	Dec
Daytime temperatures in °C/°F	30/86	30/86	31/88	31/88	31/88	31/88	31/88	31/88	30/86	31/88	30/87	29/84
Nighttime temperatures in °C/°F	23/73	23/73	24/75	24/75	24/75	25/77	25/77	24/75	24/75	24/75	24/75	23/73
Sunshine hours/day	5	6	6	6	6	6	6	6	6	5	5	4
Precipitation days/month	13	10	11	11	11	10	10	11	9	13	16	18
Water temperature in °C/°F	27/81	27/81	28/82	28/82	28/82	29/84	28/82	28/82	28/82	28/82	28/82	27/81

 Sunshine hours/day Precipitation days/month Water temperature in °C/°F

Card and admission ticket – this makes admission, for example, to the *Zoo* or *Universal Studios,* cheaper. Depending on the combination and period of validity, the pass costs from 79 S$. It can be bought at the MRT ticket counters at the Dhoby Ghaut (130 B6) *(🕮 H3)* and Orchard (129 E4) *(🕮 F2)* stations.

The *Singapore City Pass (www.singaporecitypass.com)* is valid for one to three days. It provides reduced admission fees to most attractions and cheaper tickets for tours. The price: 68.90 S$ (one day), 88.90 S$ (two days) and 159.90 S$ (three days). You can buy the pass at the Singapore Flyer observation wheel *(Tourist Hub #01–05)*.

SIGHTSEEING TOURS

Duck & Hippo Tours (adults 37, children 27 S$ | www.ducktours.com.sg) are trips in decommissioned US Army amphibious vehicles through the old part of town and then into Marina Bay – great fun, and not just for younger visitors.

The *SIA Hop-On-Bus (daily 9am–9pm | adults 25, children 15 S$ | www.siahopon.com)* operated by Singapore Airlines offers day tickets for a set route through the city in its programme. All Singapore Airlines' passengers ride for free with the *Singapore Stopover Holiday (SSH) Pass*.

You can book trips in a ● rickshaw at *www.toursinsingapore.com,* e. g. four hours through Chinatown at night including dinner for 68 S$, or one and a half hours through Little India to Arab Street with *Luxury Tours & Travel (49 S$ | tel. 67 33 28 08 | www.b2bluxurytours.com)*, and also under *www.citytours.sg* for a package including the main city sights, often combined with the ticket for the Singapore Flyer observation wheel. The *Tour East (www.toureast.net/singapore)* organisation, in cooperation with the *Chinatown Visitor Centre,* offers in-depth tours of Chinatown. The three-hour excusion *(28 S$)* features visits to the clans and homeland associations, traditional workshops where masks and combs are made, as well as to cookshops where you can take a look into the pots, *wet markets* and grocery shops.

A special experience is a ● *Singapore River Cruise (25 S$ | tel. 63 36 61 11 | www.rivercruise.com.sg)* which shows you Singapore from the water with environmentally-friendly electric bumboats.

TAXIS

All of the taxis in Singapore are air-conditioned, have an officially-sealed taximeter and are inexpensive in comparison with Britain. They can be flagged down on the street and you will find taxi ranks in front of all the main shopping centres and hotels. Telephone reservations: *Comfort & City Cab tel. 65 52 11 11; SMRT Taxi tel. 65 55 88 88; Premier tel. 63 63 68 88*; *Taxi hotline 63 42 52 22*.

Information on all taxi telephone numbers and prices can be found under *www.taxisingapore.com.* Prices and supplements are also listed on a sticker on the rear side window of the taxi. As a rule, taxi drivers do not cheat customers, but they occasionally give tourists foreign coins as change. Please note that it is compulsory to wear seat belts.

TIME

Singapore Time (SGT, no daylight saving time in summer) is eight hours ahead of GMT, twelve hours behind US Eastern Time (EST) and three hours behind Australian Eastern Time (AEST), one hour less during summer daylight saving time.

STREET ATLAS

The green line indicates the Discovery Tour 'Singapore at a glance'
The blue line indicates the other Discovery Tours
All tours are also marked in the pull-out map

Photo: View of the west side of Marina Bay

Exploring Singapore

The map on the back cover shows how the area has been sub-divided

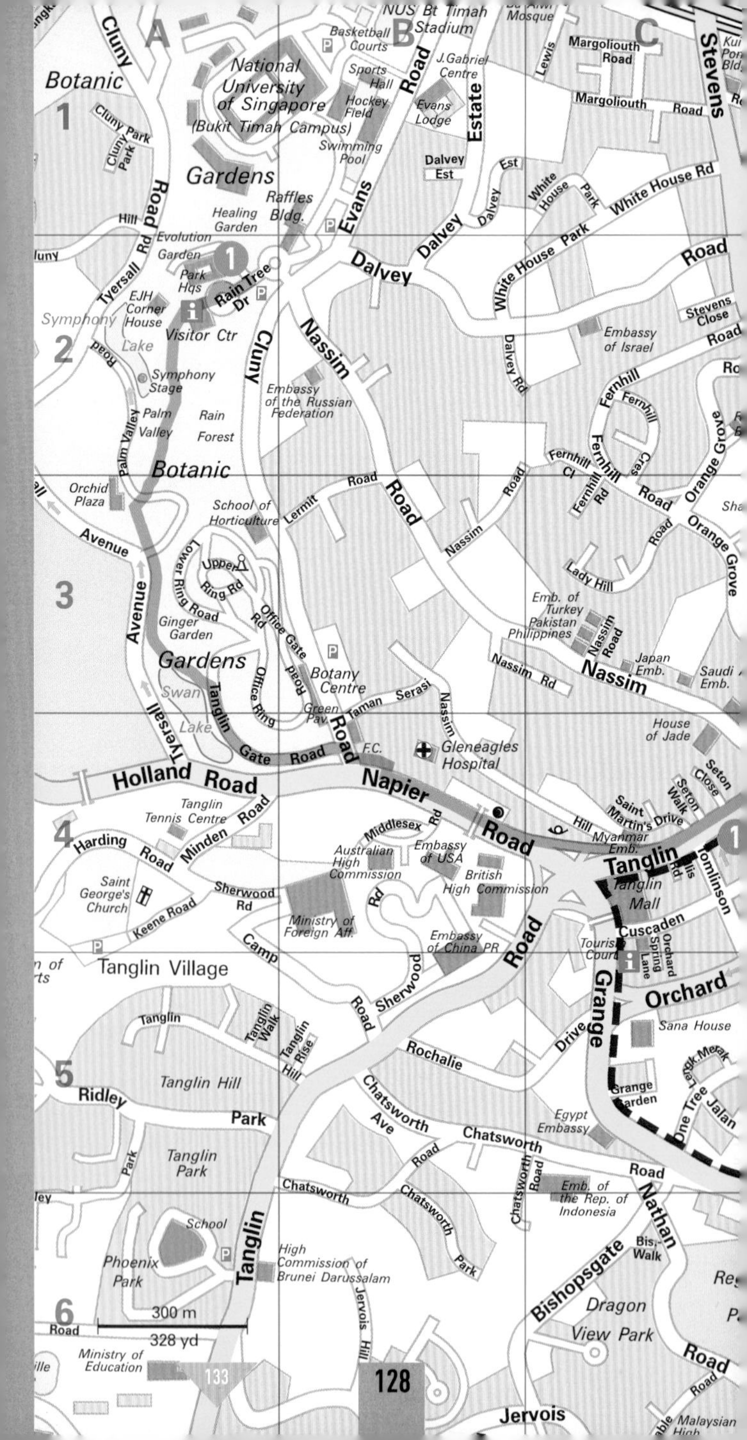
A
B
C
1
2
3
4
5
6
NUS Bt Timah Stadium
Basketball Courts
National University of Singapore (Bukit Timah Campus)
Sports Hall
Hockey Field
Swimming Pool
Raffles Bldg.
Botanic
Gardens
Healing Garden
Evolution Garden
Park Hqs
Rain Tree Dr
EJH Corner House
Visitor Ctr
Symphony Lake
Symphony Stage
Palm Valley
Rain Forest
Botanic
School of Horticulture
Upper Ring Rd
Lower Ring Road
Ginger Garden
Gardens
Swan Lake
Office Gate Rd
Office Ring Road
Botany Centre
Green Pav.
Orchid Plaza
Cluny Road
Cluny Park
Cluny Park Road
Tyersall Rd
Tyersall Avenue
Holland Road
Tanglin Gate Road
Napier Road
Evans Road
J.Gabriel Centre
Evans Lodge
Dalvey Estate
Dalvey Est
Dalvey Road
Dalvey Rd
Lewis
Margoliouth Road
Stevens Road
Stevens Close
White House Park
White House Rd
Embassy of Israel
Nassim Road
Embassy of the Russian Federation
Lermit Road
Fernhill Road
Fernhill Cres
Fernhill Cl
Fernhill Rd
Orange Grove Road
Lady Hill Road
Emb. of Turkey Pakistan Philippines
Nassim Rd
Japan Emb.
Saudi Emb.
Taman Serasi
F.C.
Gleneagles Hospital
House of Jade
Seton Close
Seton Walk
Saint Martin's Drive
Hill
Myanmar Emb.
Tanglin Road
Tanglin Mall
Tomlinson
Cuscaden
Orchard Spring Lane
Tourist Court
Orchard Road
Sana House
Grange Road
Grange Garden
One Tree Hill
Jalan Lengk.Merak
Tanglin Tennis Centre
Minden Road
Harding Road
Saint George's Church
Keene Road
Sherwood Rd
Middlesex Rd
Australian High Commission
Embassy of USA
British High Commission
Ministry of Foreign Aff.
Embassy of China PR
Camp Road
Sherwood Road
Tanglin Village
Tanglin Walk
Tanglin Rise
Tanglin Hill
Ridley Park
Tanglin Park
Rochalie Drive
Chatsworth Ave
Chatsworth Road
Chatsworth Park
Egypt Embassy
Emb. of the Rep. of Indonesia
Nathan Road
Bishopsgate
Bis. Walk
Dragon View Park
School
Phoenix Park
Tanglin
High Commission of Brunei Darussalam
Jervois Hill
Jervois
Malaysian High
Ministry of Education
300 m
328 yd
133

D
E
F
1
2
3
4
5
6
Dunearn Road
Bukit Timah
Canal
Road
Goldhill Rise
Goldhill Ave
Goldhill Drive
Goldh. View
Swiss Cottage Est
Methodist Church
School
Barker
Chancery
Jalan Pasiran
Gentle Road
Raffles Counselling Centre
Baptist Church
Robin Drive
Close
Keng Chin Road
Ewe Boon Road
Stevens Drive
City Towers
School
Evelyn Rd
Bucklev
Gilstead
Balmoral Road
Balmoral Crescent
Balmoral Park
Balm. Plaza
Jesus Crist of Latter-Day-St.
Sarkies Rd
Mai Thai Gallery
Walshe Road
Goodwood Hill
Social Devt Unit
Newton Circus
Road
NS21 Newton
Newton Rd
Raffles Girl School
Draycott Park
Draycott Dr
Stevens Rd
Goldbell Tower
School
Clemenceau Avenue
Environment Bldg
Cairnhill Garden
Cairnhill Road
Anthony Road
Peck Hay
School
Ardmore Park
Admore Pk
Tanglin Club
Hill
Tunisia Consulate
Goodwood Park
Cairnhill Art Centre
Cairnhill Circle
American Club
Royal Plaza
Delfi Orchard
Claymore Dr
Claymore Hill
Orchard Road
Claymore Towers
Royal Thai Emb.
Pacific Plaza
Scotts Road
Far East Plaza
Elizabeth
Grand Hyatt
Rise
Forum
Ming Arcade
Hilton
Internat. Bldg
Shaw Centre
Shaw House
Scotts
Nutmeg
Jln Jintan
Jln Elok
Mount Elizabeth Link
HPL House
Far East Shopping Centre
Four Seasons
Liat Tower
Marriott Hotel
Jln Lada Puteh
Jln Kayu Manis
Mount Elizabeth Hospital
Tangs Plaza
Lucky Plaza
Thong Sia Bldg
Saunders Rd
Park Rd
Wheelock Place
ION
Orchard
Mount Elizabeth Road
Bideford Road
Tong Bldg.
The Paragon
Al- Falah Mosque
Cuscaden Walk
NS22 Orchard
Wisma Atria
Orchard Parksuites
Takashimaya Center
Wellington Bldg.
Hullet Road
Starhub Centre
Anguilla
Tupai
Paterson Road
Ngee Ann City
Orchard Turn
Link
The Heeren
Mandarin Sh. Arcade
School
Emerald Hill
Centre Point
Tree Hill
Kelawar
Arnap
SIM
Paterson Centre
Boulevard
Orchard Link
Cineleisure
Faber House
Orchard Bldg
Lengkok Angsa
Paterson Hill
International Schools
Somerset Rd
Somerset
Orchard Central
Power Bldg
NS23 Somerset
Skate Park
Grange Road
Grange Rd
Devonshire Rd
Exeter Road
High Commisson of India
Comcentre
Ministry of Education Teachers Network
Hoot Kiam Road
Irwell Bank Road
Leonie Hill
Tiverton Lane
Dublin Rd
Devonshire Bldg
Tong Xian Ting Temple
Tai Wah Bldg
Lloyd Gardens
Lloyd Road
Baptist Church
Muslim Cemetery
River Valley Grove
Saint Thomas Walk
Killiney Road
CGH Bldg.
Jalan Mutiara
Kaypoh Road
River Valley Road
The Tiara
The Cosmopolitan
St Bernadette Church
Shanghai
Kim
134

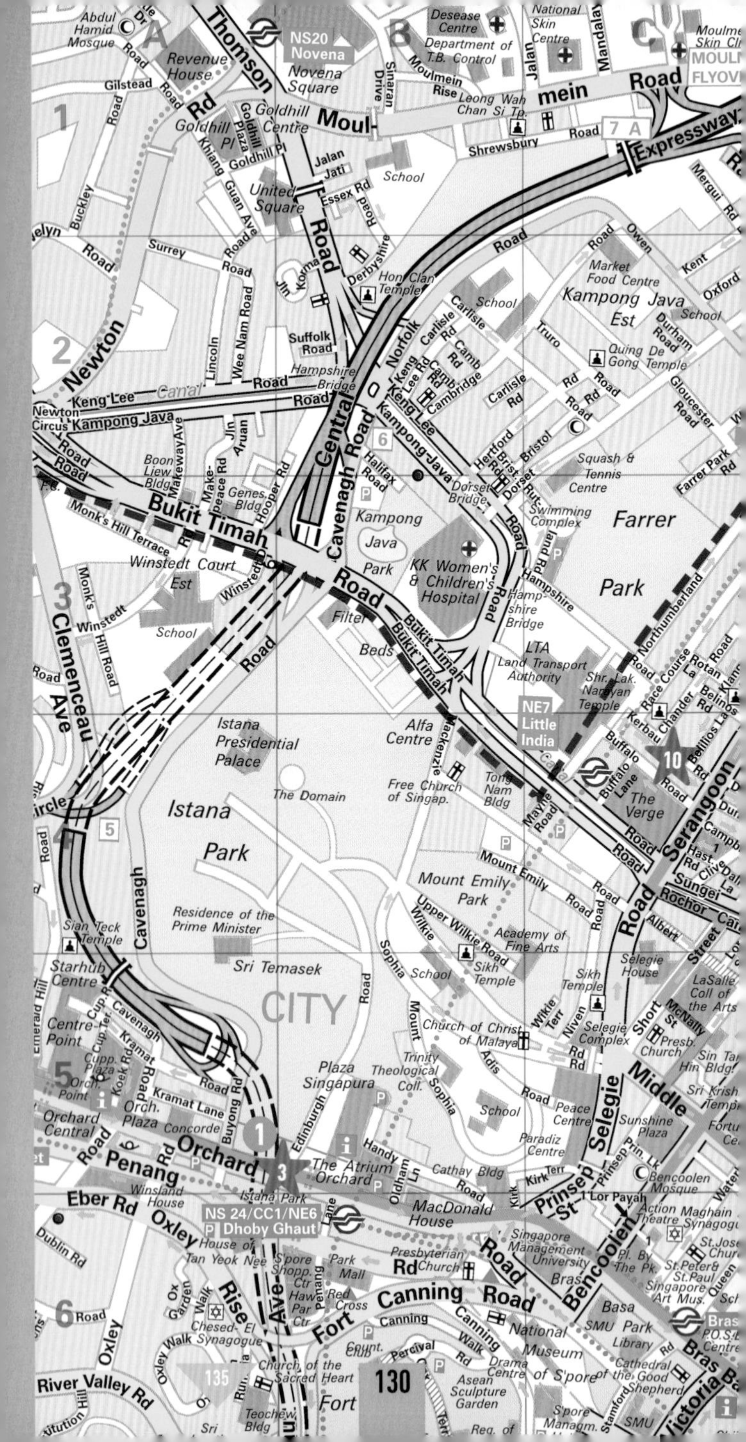
A
B
C
1
2
3
4
5
6
Abdul Hamid Mosque
Revenue House
Thomson Rd
NS20 Novena
Novena Square
Desease Centre
Department of T.B. Control
National Skin Centre
Moulmein Road
Moulmein Rise
Sinaran Drive
Jalan
Mandalay
MOULMEIN FLYOVER
Leong Wah Chan Si Tp.
Shrewsbury Road
7 A
Expressway
Gilstead Road
Goldhill Centre
Goldhill Plaza
Goldhill Pl
Khiang Guan Ave
Jalan Jati
School
United Square
Essex Rd
Buckley Road
Surrey Road
Road
Jln Korma
Derbyshire Road
Hon Clan Temple
Mergui Rd
Owen Road
Market Food Centre
Kent
Oxford
Kampong Java Est
School
Durham Road
Truro
Quing De Gong Temple
Gloucester Road
Newton
Lincoln
Wee Nam Road
Suffolk Road
Hampshire Bridge
Keng Lee Road
Canal
Kampong Java Road
Newton Circus
Central
Cavenagh Road
Norfolk
Carlisle Rd
Camb Rd
Cambridge
Keng Lee Rd
Hertford Rd
Brist.
Bristol
Dorset Rd
Squash & Tennis Centre
Farrer Park Rd
Boon Liew Bldg
Makeway Ave
Makepeace Rd
Jln Aruan
Genes. Bldg
Hooper Rd
Halifax Road
Kampong Java Park
Dorset Bridge
Rut. Road
Swimming Complex
Farrer Park
Bukit Timah Road
Monk's Hill Terrace
Winstedt Court Est
Winstedt Rd
KK Women's & Children's Hospital
Hampshire Road
Hampshire Bridge
Northumberland
Monk's Hill Road
Clemenceau Ave
School
Filter Beds
Bukit Timah
LTA Land Transport Authority
Shr. Lak. Narayan Temple
Race Course La
Rotan La
Belinos Rd
Kerbau
Chander
NE7 Little India
Buffalo Lane
Bellilios La
10
The Verge
Serangoon Road
Istana Presidential Palace
The Domain
Alfa Centre
Mackenzie
Free Church of Singap.
Tong Nam Bldg
Mayne Road
Istana Park
5
Mount Emily Road
Mount Emily Park
Upper Wilkie Road
Wilkie
Academy of Fine Arts
Sikh Temple
Residence of the Prime Minister
Sri Temasek
Sian Teck Temple
Cavenagh
Starhub Centre
Sophia Road
School
CITY
Selegie House
Sikh Temple
Rochor Canal
Albert Street
Sungei Rd
LaSalle Coll of the Arts
McNally St
Centre Point
Cavenagh Road
Kramat Road
Cupp. Plaza
Koek Rd
Orch. Point
Kramat Lane
Buyong Rd
Church of Christ of Malaya
Trinity Theological Coll.
Mount Sophia
Wilkie Terr
Niven Rd
Selegie Complex
Short St
Presb. Church
Sin Tai Hin Bldg
Plaza Singapura
Edinburgh Road
Adis Road
School
Peace Centre
Selegie
Middle Road
Sunshine Plaza
Sri Krishna Temple
Orchard Central
Orch. Plaza
Concorde
Orchard Road
Penang Rd
1
3
The Atrium Orchard
Handy Road
Oldham Ln
Cathay Bldg
Paradiz Centre
Kirk Terr
Prinsep St
Prinsep Lk
Bencoolen Mosque
Winsland House
Eber Rd
Oxley Rise
Dublin Rd
Istana Park
NS 24/CC1/NE6 Dhoby Ghaut
Lane
MacDonald House
1 Lor Payah
Action Theatre
Maghain Synagogue
House of Tan Yeok Nee
S'pore Shopp. Ctr
Penang
Park Mall
Presbyterian Church
Rd
Singapore Management University
Bras Basah
Bencoolen
Pl. By The Pk.
St. Joseph Church
St. Peter & St. Paul
Singapore Art Mus.
Queen
Ox Garden Walk
Chesed-El Synagogue
Hawk Par Ctr
Red Cross
Fort Canning Road
Canning
Canning Walk
National Museum of S'pore
Basa SMU Park Library
Oxley Road
Oxley Walk
River Valley Rd
135
Church of the Sacred Heart
Count. Club
Percival Rd
Drama Centre
Asean Sculpture Garden
Cathedral of the Good Shepherd
Stamford Rd
Bras Basah
P.O.S.B. Centre
Victoria
Teochew Bldg
Fort
S'pore Managm.
SMU
130

D
E
F
1
2
3
4
5
6
Singapore Vocational Institute
7 C
Eye Hospital
Balestier
Ceylon Sports Club
S'pore Indian Assoc.
S'pore Chinese Sports Club
Rangoon
School
McNair
HIS Sanct. Serv.
S'pore Khalsa Assoc.
Central Sikh Temple
Road
Kwong Wai Siu Free Hospital
Serangoon
Rd
Boon Keng
Bendemeer Mall
NE9
Boon Keng
Road
Kallang Bahru
Kallang Tengah
Bahru
F.C.
Mkt. F.C.
Peta-ling Rd
Kempas Rd
Tronoh Rd
Kempas
Idris
Lavender
Bendemeer
Hiap Huat House
Jalan Lembah Kallang
Cyber Hub
Road
Sing Ave
Sing Joo Walk
Joo Avenue
Civil Service Clubhouse
Sri V. Temple
Tamil Malar
Chinese Temple
Sakaya Muni Buddha Gaya Temple
Tessensohn
Race Course
Sri Sivan Temple
Sri Srinivasa Perumal Temple
Beatty Road
Sch
Sturdee Rd
Wu De Bldg
Thekchen Chöling
Jalan Besar
Eminent Plaza
Curch of Victory
Kallang
GEO Technique Bldg
Kallang Junction
Kallang Avenue
Star-light Rd
Perumal Rd
Petain Rd
Marne Rd
Kitchener
Road
Rd
Sturdee Rd
Est
Foch Rd
Road
Casket
City Square Mall
Flanders Sq
Link
Somme Rd
Road
Hamilton Rd
Horne
Cavan Road
Burmah Rd
Birch Rd
Angullia Mosque
Kitchener
Serangoon Plaza
Mustafa Centre
Verdun Rd
Sam Leong Rd
Football Assoc of S'pore
Allen Rd
Jln Besar Stadium
Avenue
Creative Centre
F.C.
Avenue
Padang Jeringau
Tai Pei Buddhist Centre
Syed Alwi
Desker
Rowell
Baboo La
Hindoo Rd
Road
Road
Besar
Plumer Rd
Tyrwhitt Rd
Jln Besar Plaza
School
Maude
Road
Road
King George's
French Rd
French Road
Penhas Rd
Road
Road
Jellicoe
St
Kallang Rd
Sri Manmathan Temple
EW11
Lavender
Kampong
Nam Lock
Kampong Kapor
Chitty Rd
Hindoo Rd
Road
Jalan
New World Ctr.
Townshend
Jalan
F.C.
Kelan. La
Kelan.
Berseh
Road
ICA Bldg.
Crawford Bridge
Crawford
Upper Weld Rd
Kelantan
Polyclinic
Road
Syed Alwi Bridge
Street
Victoria Bridge
Eng Cheong Tower
Bugis
Road
Road
Larut Rd
Pitt Rd
Weld Rd
Abdul Gaffoor Mosque
Rochor Canal
Jalan Kubor
Muslim Cem
Old Malay Cem
Jalan
Hong Wen Sch
Crawford Lane
Bus Terminal
St
Sim Lim Tower
Sungei
Arab St
Victoria La
School
Jln Klapa
Jln Kledek
Plaza Cinema Textile Ctr
Sch.
Ban San St
Bus Term.
Ophir
Rd
Jln Pisang
Jln Pinang
Istana Kg Glam Malay Her. Ctr.
Aliwal
Sultan Plaza
Minto Road
Key-point
Hajjah Fatimah Mosque
Road
Golden Mile Complex
Golden Theatre
Rochor Centre
Albert
Rochor
Queen
Wholesale Centre
Sultan Mosque
Kandahar St
Muscat St
Sultan
Pahang St
Street
Golden Mile Tower
Java Rd
Johore
Victoria
Raffles Hospital
Blanco Court
Bridge
Haji La
Bali La
Baghdad St
Gate
Bussorah St
The Concourse
Highway
CC5
Nicoll Highway
Street
Fu Lu Shou Cpl
EW12/DT14
Bugis
Bugis Street
North
Parkview Square
Street
Beach
The Furniture Mall
Parkroyal
Promenade
Cheng Yan Pl
PARCO Bugis Junction
Manila St
The Plaza
Republic Avenue
Marina
Malabar St
Hylam St
Rd
Bern. St
Beach La
Tan Quee Lan
St
Road
The Gateway
Liang Seah St
S'pore Finance House
Nat. Library
Road
Beach
Kimetal Bldg.
Shaw Towers
Nicoll
Road
Road
300 m
328 yd
Bras Basah Cpl
Purvis St
Mus. of Toys
Seah Street
Beach Centre
Raffles Hotel
Church La
Suntec City Mall

137

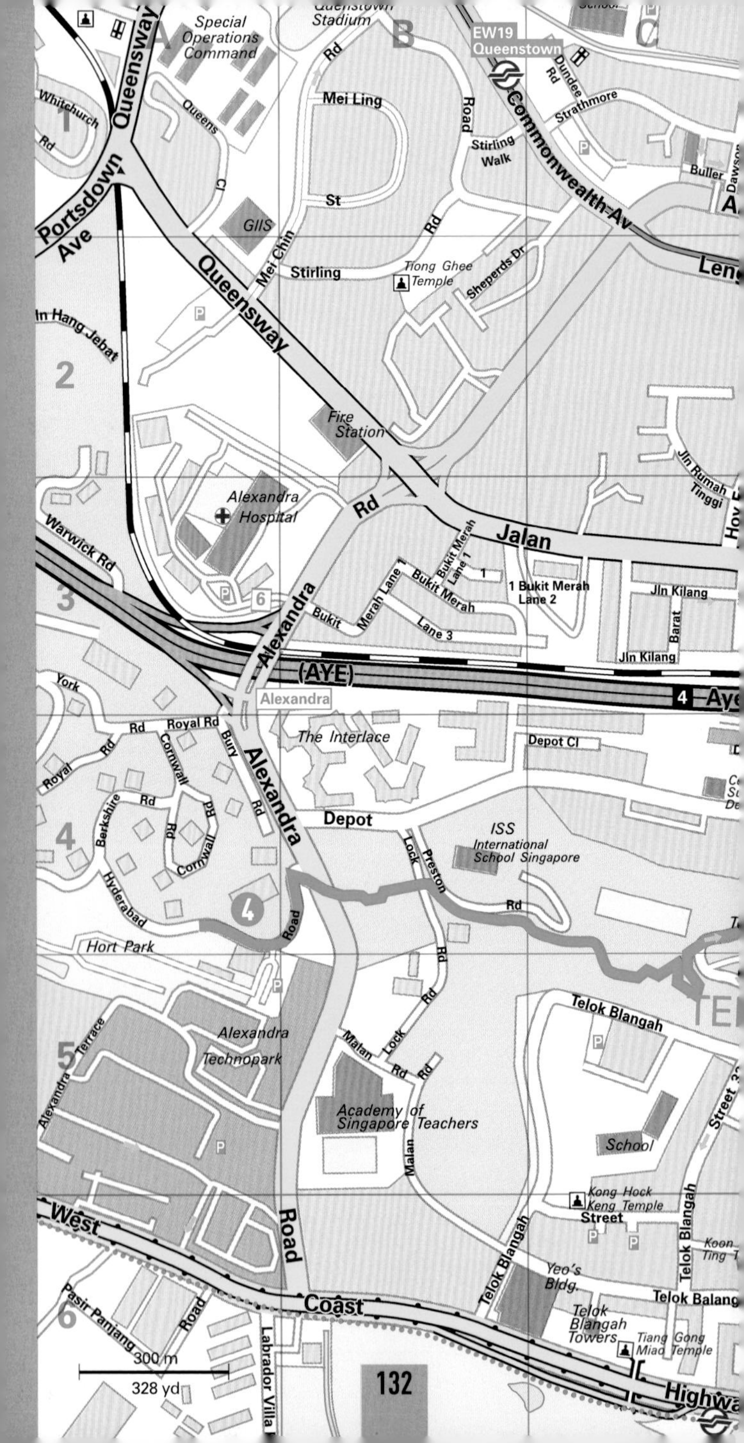

Stadium
Special Operations Command
EW19 Queenstown
Dundee Rd
Whitchurch Rd
Queensway
Queens Cl
Mei Ling St
Road
Stirling Walk
Commonwealth Av
Strathmore
Buller
Dawson
Portsdown Ave
GIIS
Mei Chin Rd
Stirling
Tiong Ghee Temple
Sheperds Dr
Jln Hang Jebat
Queensway
Fire Station
Jln Rumah Tinggi
Alexandra Hospital
Rd
Jalan
Warwick Rd
Bukit Merah Lane 1
1 Bukit Merah Lane 2
Jln Kilang
Bukit Merah Lane 1
Bukit Merah Lane 3
Alexandra
Barat
Jln Kilang
(AYE)
4
Alexandra
York
Rd
Royal Rd
Royal Rd
Cornwall
Bury Rd
Alexandra
The Interlace
Depot Cl
Berkshire Rd
Rd
Cornwall Rd
Depot
ISS International School Singapore
Lock
Preston
Rd
Hyderabad
4
Road
Hort Park
Rd
Telok Blangah
Alexandra Technopark
Alexandra Terrace
Malan Rd
Lock Rd
Rd
Academy of Singapore Teachers
Malan
School
Street 32
Kong Hock Keng Temple
Street
Telok Blangah
West
Road
Telok Blangah
Yeo's Bldg.
Coast
Telok Balang
Telok Blangah Towers
Tiang Gong Miao Temple
Pasir Panjang Road
Labrador Villa
300 m
328 yd

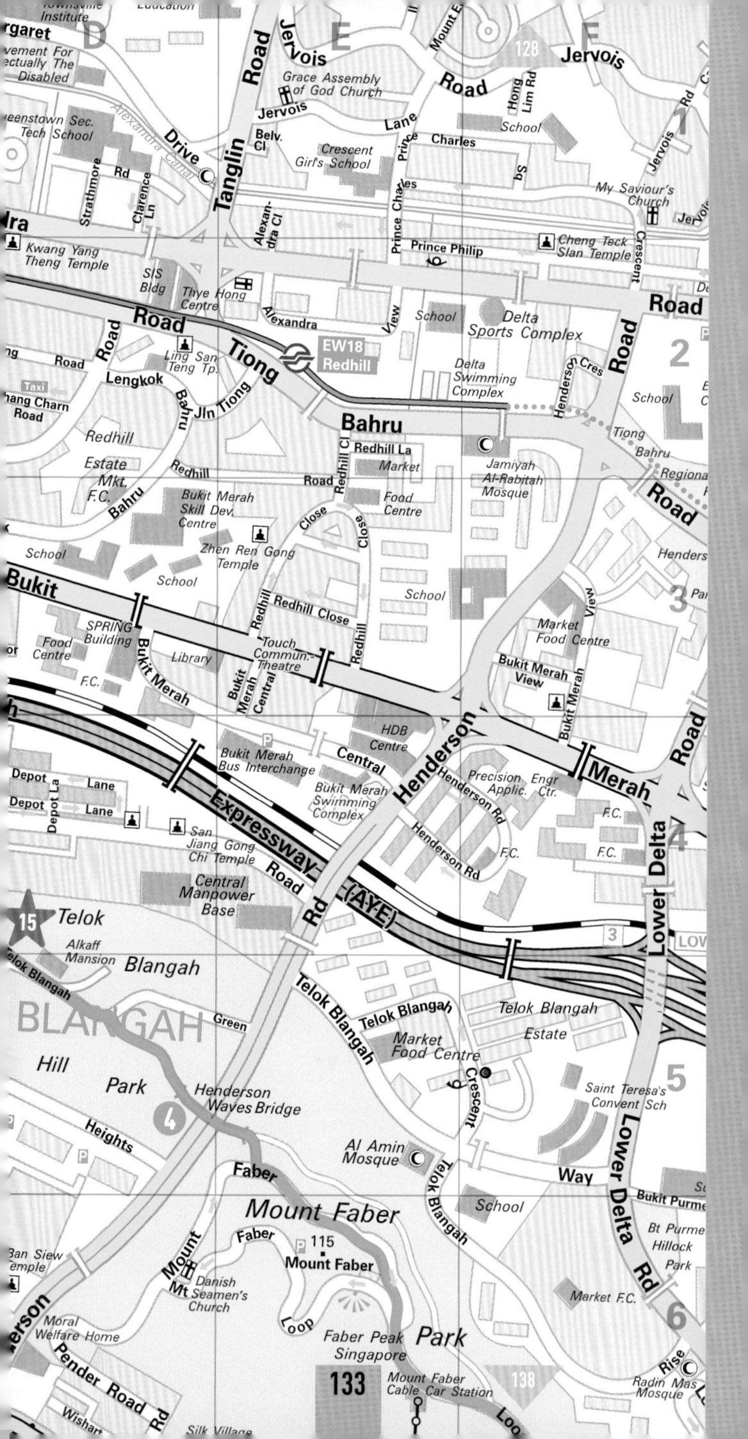

Jervois Road
Grace Assembly of God Church
Jervois Lane
Hong Lim Rd
School
Charles
Prince Charles
Belv. Cl
Crescent Girl's School
Tanglin Road
Alexandra Canal
Drive
Strathmore Rd
Clarence Ln
Alexandra Cl
Prince Charles Crescent
My Saviour's Church
Kwang Yang Theng Temple
Prince Philip
Cheng Teck Slan Temple
Crescent
SIS Bldg
Thye Hong Centre
Alexandra View
School
Delta Sports Complex
Road
Tiong Bahru Road
Ling San Teng Tp.
EW18 Redhill
Delta Swimming Complex
Henderson Cres
Lengkok Bahru
Jln Tiong
Taxi
Redhill Estate Mkt. F.C.
Redhill Road
Redhill La
Market
Jamiyah Al-Rabitah Mosque
Redhill Cl
Food Centre
Bukit Merah Skill Dev. Centre
Close
Zhen Ren Gong Temple
School
Henderson
Bukit Merah View
SPRING Building
Food Centre
Library
Redhill Close
Touch Commun. Theatre
Market Food Centre
Bukit Merah View
Bukit Merah Central
F.C.
HDB Centre
Bukit Merah Bus Interchange
Central
Henderson Rd
Precision Applic.
Engr Ctr.
Merah
Depot Lane
Depot La
Bukit Merah Swimming Complex
San Jiang Gong Chi Temple
Expressway (AYE)
F.C.
Lower Delta
Central Manpower Base
Telok Blangah
Alkaff Mansion
BLANGAH
Green
Telok Blangah Estate
Market Food Centre
Crescent
Hill Park
Henderson Waves Bridge
Heights
Saint Teresa's Convent Sch
Al Amin Mosque
Way
Faber
Mount Faber
School
Bukit Purmei
Bt Purmei Hillock Park
Ban Siew Temple
115
Mount
Danish Seamen's Church
Market F.C.
Moral Welfare Home
Loop
Faber Peak Singapore
Park
Pender Road
Mount Faber Cable Car Station
Rise
Radin Mas Mosque
Wishart
Silk Village
128
138
D E F
1 2 3 4 5 6
15

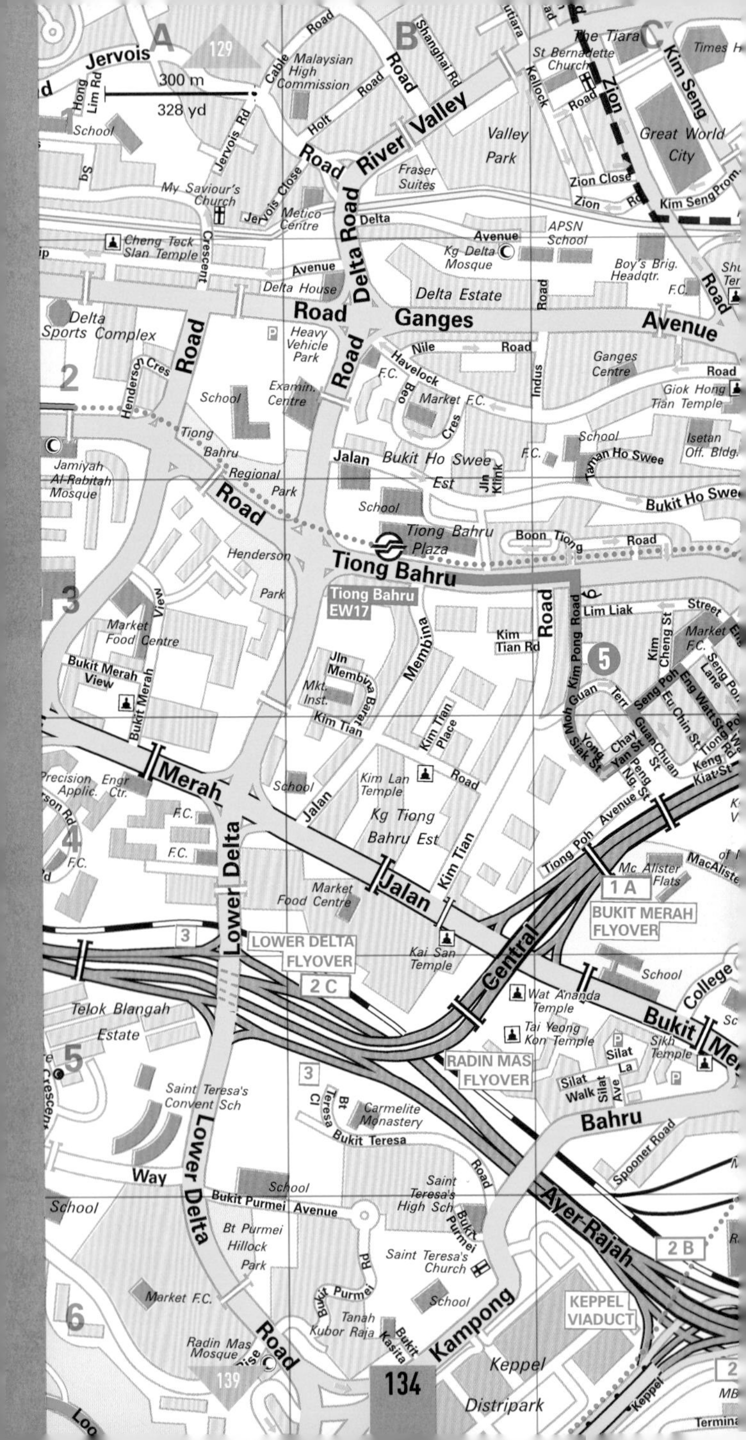
A
B
C
129
300 m
328 yd
Jervois
Hong Lim Rd
School
Cable Road
Malaysian High Commission
Holt Road
Shanghai Rd
Road
River Valley
Valley Park
Fraser Suites
Jervois Rd
Jervois Close
My Saviour's Church
Metico Centre
Delta Road
Delta Avenue
Kg Delta Mosque
APSN School
Cheng Teck Slan Temple
Crescent
Avenue
Delta House
Delta Estate
Ganges Avenue
Road
The Tiara
St Bernadette Church
Kellock Road
Zion Road
Kim Seng
Great World City
Zion Close
Kim Seng Prom.
Times H
Boy's Brig. Headqtr.
F.C.
Delta Sports Complex
Henderson Cres
Road
Heavy Vehicle Park
Nile Road
Havelock Road
Beo Cres
Market F.C.
Examin. Centre
School
Indus Road
Ganges Centre
Giok Hong Tian Temple
Tiong Bahru Regional Park
Road
Jalan Bukit Ho Swee
Est
Jln Klink
Taman Ho Swee
School
F.C.
Isetan Off. Bldg.
Bukit Ho Swee
Jamiyah Al-Rabitah Mosque
School
Tiong Bahru Plaza
Boon Tiong Road
Tiong Bahru
Tiong Bahru EW17
Henderson Park
View
Market Food Centre
Bukit Merah View
Bukit Merah
Membina
Jln Membina Barat
Mkt. Inst.
Kim Tian
Kim Tian Rd
Road
Lim Liak Street
Kim Pong Road
Kim Cheng St
Market F.C.
Seng Poh Lane
Moh Guan Terr
Seng Poh
Eng Watt St
Eu Chin St
Guan Chuan St
Yong Siak St
Chay Yan St
Peng Ng. St
Tiong Poh Rd
Keng Kiat St
Kim Tian Place
Kim Lan Temple
Road
Precision Engr Applic. Ctr.
Merah
School
Jalan
Kg Tiong Bahru Est
Kim Tian
Tiong Poh Avenue
F.C.
F.C.
Lower Delta
Jalan
Market Food Centre
Mc Alister Flats
MacAlister
1 A
BUKIT MERAH FLYOVER
3
LOWER DELTA FLYOVER
2 C
Kai San Temple
Central
School
College
Wat Ananda Temple
Bukit Merah
Telok Blangah Estate
Tai Yeong Kon Temple
Sikh Temple
Silat La
Silat Walk
Silat Ave
RADIN MAS FLYOVER
3
Bt Teresa Cl
Carmelite Monastery
Bukit Teresa
Bahru
Spooner Road
Saint Teresa's Convent Sch
Crescent
Way
School
Lower Delta
Road
School
Bukit Purmei Avenue
Saint Teresa's High Sch
Bukit Purmei
Ayer-Rajah
Bt Purmei Hillock Park
Saint Teresa's Church
2 B
Market F.C.
Purmei Rd
School
Bukit Purmei
Tanah Kubor Raja
Bukit Kasita
Kampong
KEPPEL VIADUCT
Radin Mas Mosque
Rise
Road
139
Keppel Distripark
Keppel
Termina
Loo

River Valley Road
Church of the Sacred Heart
Battle Box
Fort Canning Park
Fort Canning Centre
Fort Canning Service Reservoir
River Valley Swimming Complex
130
Institution Hill
Aspen Heights
Teochew Bldg
Sri Thendayuthapani Temple
Tank Road
Singapore Buddhist Lodge
Hong San See Temple
Tong Watt Road
United Engineer's Square
Shell House
UE Shopping Mall
River Valley Green
Hock Giap Warehouse
Unity Street
Kim Seng Park
Robertson Quay
Rodyk Street
Saiboo St
Nanson Rd
Martin
Arnasalam Chetty Rd
Mohamed Sultan Road
Merbau Rd
Theatre Works
Print Inst.
Repertory Theatre
Clemenceau Bridge
Ord Bridge
Liang Court
The Foundry
The Cannery
Traders Market
Jiak Kim Street
Rivergate
Singapore River
The Institute Gallery
Alkaff Bridge
Alkaff Quay
The Quayside
Earle Q.
Clemenceau Ave
Merchant Loop
Riverside Point
Clarke St
North Boat Quay
NE5 Cl. Quay
Read Bridge
Tan Si Chong Su Temple
Magazine Road
Fisher St
Merchant Rd
The Central
Outram Road
Havelock Rd
Central Mall
Solo St
Cumming St
Angus St
Keng Cheow St
Melaka Mosq.
Min. of Manpower
New Mkt Road
Tew Chew St
Thong Chai Bldg
Sea Care Bldg
Jalan Minyak
Jln Kukoh
York Hill Estate
Manhattan House
Upper Cross St
Hav. Rd
Tong Chai Medical Inst.
North Canal Rd
Hong Lim Park
Pearl's Hill Road
Pearl's Hill Terrace
Subordinate Courts
Havelock Sq.
People's Park Centre
Upp Pickering St
Upper Hokien St
School
York Hill
San Centre
Police Bldg
OG Bldg
Chinatown Pt
Fook Hai Bldg
YWCA Outram Centre
Pearl's Hill
Police Natl. Service HQ
F.C.
NE4/DT19 Chinatown
Institute of Health
Outram Hill
Pearl's Hill Reservoir
City Park
Park Rd
People's Park Complex
Mosque Street
Cross St
Chin Chew St
1 B
Outram Park
Chinatown Herit. Ctr.
Temple St
Jamae Mosque
Smith St
Pagoda St
Trengganu St
Sri Mariamman Temple
Club St
Pearl Bank Apartment
Chinatown Complex
Outram Flyover
National Heart Centre
Pearl's Hill
Oriental Plaza
Sago St
Eu Yang Sun
EW16/NE3 Outram Park
Pearl's Centre
Kreta Ayer Road
Kreta Ayer People's Th.
Banda St
Sago La
Ann Siang Rd
Ann S. Hill
Third Hospital Ave
National Eye Centre
Hospital Ave
Eu Tong Sen
Hindu Temple
Kreta Ayer Ctr.
Spr. St
Dick. St
South Bridge Road
Erskine Rd
Thian Hock Keng Temp.
Singapore General Hospital
National Dental Centre
National Cancer Ctr.
Second Hospital Ave
New Bridge Rd
Teo Hong Rd
Bukit Pasoh Rd
Duxton Plain
Keong Saik
Jiak Ch. Rd
Teck Lim Road
Maxwell Rd. F. Ctr.
Kadayanallur St
Amoy St
Siang Cho Keong Temp.
Jinrikisha Station
Kreta Ayer Clin.
Mur. St
Maxwell House
Maxwell Road
URA Centre
City Gallery Annex Bldg
Telok Ayer
Nurses Quarters
Central Circus
Bus Terminal
Hospital Drive
Bridge Rd
Cantonment Road
Chinatown Plaza
Duxton Hill
Duxton Road
Cook St
Street
Police Cantonment Complex
Baba House
Craig Road
Veterinary Centre
School of Nursing
St. Matthew's Church
French Bus. Centre
White House
Neil Road
Park
Maritime House
Phoo Thor Chi Temple
Pager Market F.C.
Wallich St
EW15 Tanjong Pagar
Blair Rd
Everton Road
Everton Park
Tanjong Pagar Plaza
Tras St
Peck Seah St
Choon Guan St
International Plaza
Anson Road
Spottiswoode Park
Port Worker's Union House
Gop. St
Seng Wong Beo Temple
Parsi Rd
MAS Bldg
Shenton Way
Park Road
Cantonment Cl.
Corrupt Pract. Inv. Bureau
Tan Kit
Kee Seng St
Hoe Chiang Rd
Keppel Towers
Union Bldg
Enggor Street
Anson Centre
Misti Rd
Palmer Rd
Realty Centre
Apex Tower
Shenton Bldg
Hock Teck See Temple
Tanjong Pagar Station
Malayan Railway
Spottiswoode Park Road
Cantonment Link
Euro Asia Ctr.
Lim Teck Kim Road
Jit Poh Bldg
RCL Centre
Bernam St
IBM Towers
South Point
Expressway (AYE)
Keppel Road
Tanjong Pagar Complex
Anson Rd
Keppel Workshop
Tanjong Pagar Distripark
Keppel Avenue
Termi

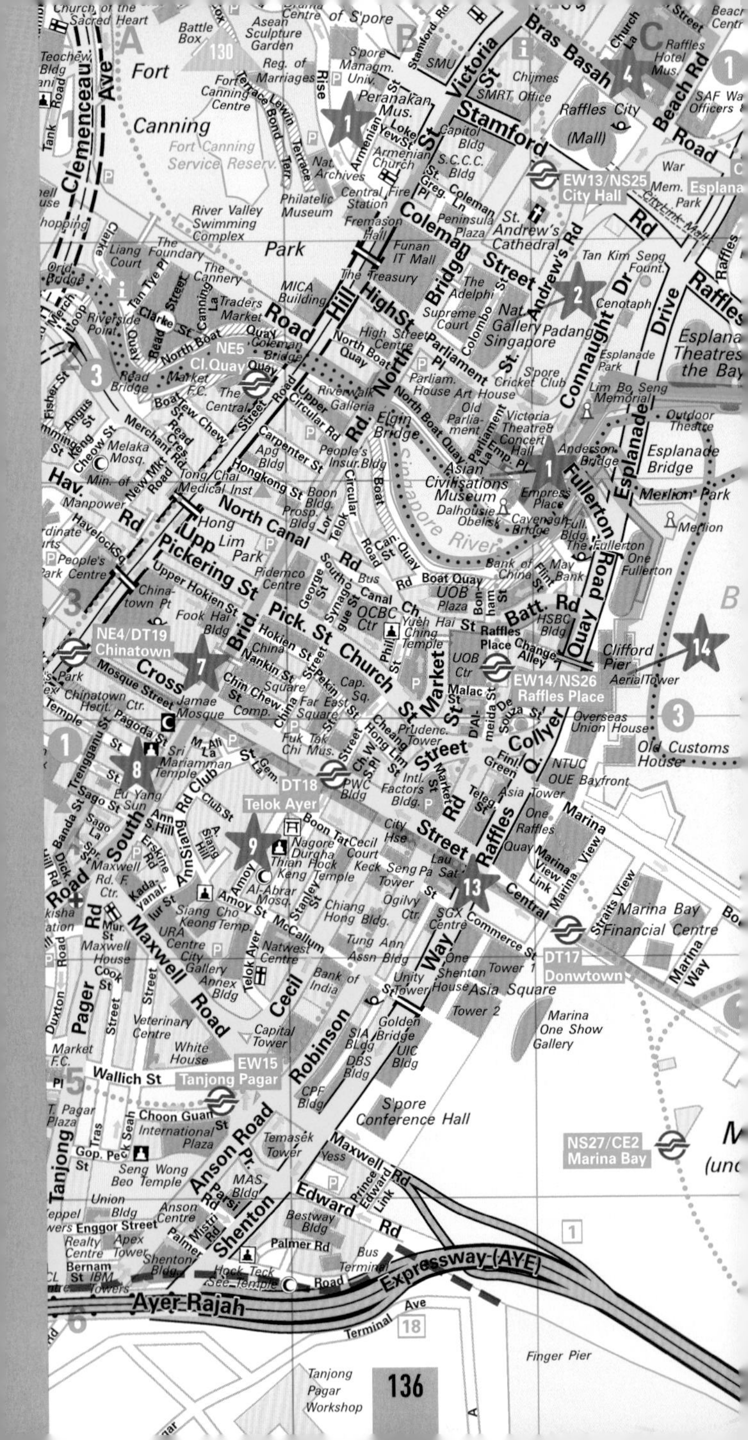

Church of the Sacred Heart
Battle Box
Asean Sculpture Garden
Centre of S'pore
130
Fort Canning
Teochew Bldg
Clemenceau Ave
Fort Canning Centre
Reg. of Marriages
S'pore Managm. Univ.
SMU
Stamford Rd
Victoria St
Bras Basah
Church La
Raffles Hotel Mus.
Beach Rd
SAF Warrant Officers
Chijmes
SMRT Office
Raffles City (Mall)
Stamford
Canning
Fort Canning Service Reserv.
Peranakan Mus.
Loke Yew St
Armenian Church
Armenian St
Capitol Bldg
S.C.C.C. Bldg
Nat. Archives
EW13/NS25 City Hall
War Mem. Park
Esplanade
Philatelic Museum
Central Fire Station
St. Greg. Pl
Coleman Ln
Peninsula Plaza
St. Andrew's Cathedral
Rd
River Valley Swimming Complex
Fremason Hall
Coleman Street
Park
Liang Court
The Foundary
The Cannery
Funan IT Mall
The Treasury
Tan Kim Seng Fount.
MICA Building
Traders Market
Tan Tye Pl
Clarke St
Riverside Point
Clarke Quay
Read Street
Canning La
Road
Hill
High St
The Adelphi
Supreme Court
Bridge
Nat. Gallery Singapore
St. Andrew's Rd
Padang
Cenotaph
Connaught Dr
Drive
Raffles
Esplanade Theatres on the Bay
North Boat Quay
Coleman Bridge
High Street Centre
North Boat Quay
Parliament Pl
Colombo
Esplanade Park
NE5 Cl. Quay
Read Bridge
Market F.C.
The Central
Street
North
Parliam. House Art House
S'pore Cricket Club
Lim Bo Seng Memorial
Fisher St
Angus St
Keng Cheow St
Merchant Rd
Melaka Mosq.
Upper Circular Rd
Riverwalk Galleria
Carpenter St
Apg Bldg
People's Insur. Bldg
Elgin Bridge
Old Parliament
Victoria Theatre & Concert Hall
Outdoor Theatre
Esplanade Bridge
Anderson Bridge
Asian Civilisations Museum
Empress Place
Fullerton
Esplanade
Merlion Park
Hav. Rd
Min. of Manpower
New Mkt Road
Tong Chai Medical Inst
Hongkong St
Boon Prosp. Bldg
Circular
Boat
Singapore River
Dalhousie Obelisk
Cavenagh Bridge
Full. Bldg.
The Fullerton
Merlion
One Fullerton
Havelock Sq.
People's Park Centre
North Canal
Hong Lim Park
Upp Pickering St
Telok Road
Can. St
Quay
Bank of China
May Bank
Flint St
Road
Rd
Upper Hokien St
Pidemco Centre
George St
South Canal
Bus Rd
Boat Quay
UOB Plaza
Bonham St
Batt. Rd
HSBC Bldg
Quay
China-town Pt
Fook Hai Bldg
Brid. Rd
Pick. St
Synagogue St
OCBC Ctr
Ch. St
Yueh Hai Ching Temple
Raffles Place
Change Alley
Clifford Pier
NE4/DT19 Chinatown
Hokien St
China St
Church
Phil St
UOB Ctr
EW14/NS26 Raffles Place
Aerial Tower
Cross
Mosque Street
Nankin St
Street
Pekin St
Cap. Sq.
Market St
Malac St
D'Almeida St
De Souza St
Overseas Union House
Park
Chinatown Herit. Ctr.
Jamae Mosque
Chin Chew St
Square Comp.
China St
Far East Square
Cheang Hong Lim St
Prudenc. Tower
Collyer Q.
Old Customs House
Temple St
Pagoda St
M. Ali La
Fuk Tak Chi Mus.
Street
Ch. W. S. Pl
Street
Fini Green
NTUC
OUE Bayfront
Trengganu St
Sri Mariamman Temple
Gem. La
DT18 Telok Ayer
PWC Bldg
Intl. Factors Bldg.
Market St
Rd
Asia Tower
Sago St
Eu Yang Sun
Club St
Ann Siang Rd
Teleg. St
Raffles
One Raffles Quay
Marina View
Banda St
Sago La
South
Ann S. Hill
A. Siang Hill
Boon Tat
City Hse
Street
Marina View Link
Dick. Rd
Spr. St
Erskine Rd
Nagore Durgha
Cecil Court
Lau Pa Sat
Straits View
Marina Bay Financial Centre
Maxwell Rd. F. Ctr.
Kada-yanal-lur St
Thian Hock Keng Temple
Keck Seng Tower
Road
Amoy St
Al-Abrar Mosq.
Stanley St
Ogilvy Ctr.
Central
Mur. St
Siang Cho Keong Temp.
Chiang Hong Bldg.
SGX Centre
Commerce St
Maxwell House
URA Centre
McCallum
Tung Ann Assn Bldg
Natwest Centre
DT17 Downtown
Marina Way
Cook St
City Gallery Annex Bldg
Telok Ayer
Bank of India
Way
One Shenton
Tower 1
Duxton Road
Pager Rd
Street
Maxwell
Road
Cecil
Unity House
St Tower
Asia Square Tower 2
Veterinary Centre
Capital Tower
Golden Bridge
Marina One Show Gallery
Market F.C.
White House
Robinson
SIA Bldg
UIC Bldg
DBS Bldg
Wallich St
EW15 Tanjong Pagar
T. Pagar Plaza
Choon Guan St
CPF Bldg
S'pore Conference Hall
Tanjong
Tras St
Keck Seah
International Plaza
Anson Road
Temasek Tower
Maxwell Rd
NS27/CE2 Marina Bay
Gop. Peck St
Seng Wong Beo Temple
Yess
Pr.
MAS Bldg
Prince Edward Link
Union Bldg
Parsi Rd
Shenton
Edward
Keppel Towers
Enggor Street
Anson Centre
Realty Centre
Apex Tower
Mistri Rd
Bestway Bldg
Rd
1
Bernam St
Palmer
Shenton Bldg.
Palmer Rd
Bus Terminal
IBM Towers
Hock Teck See Temple
Road
Expressway (AYE)
Ayer Rajah
Terminal Ave
18
Finger Pier
Tanjong Pagar Workshop

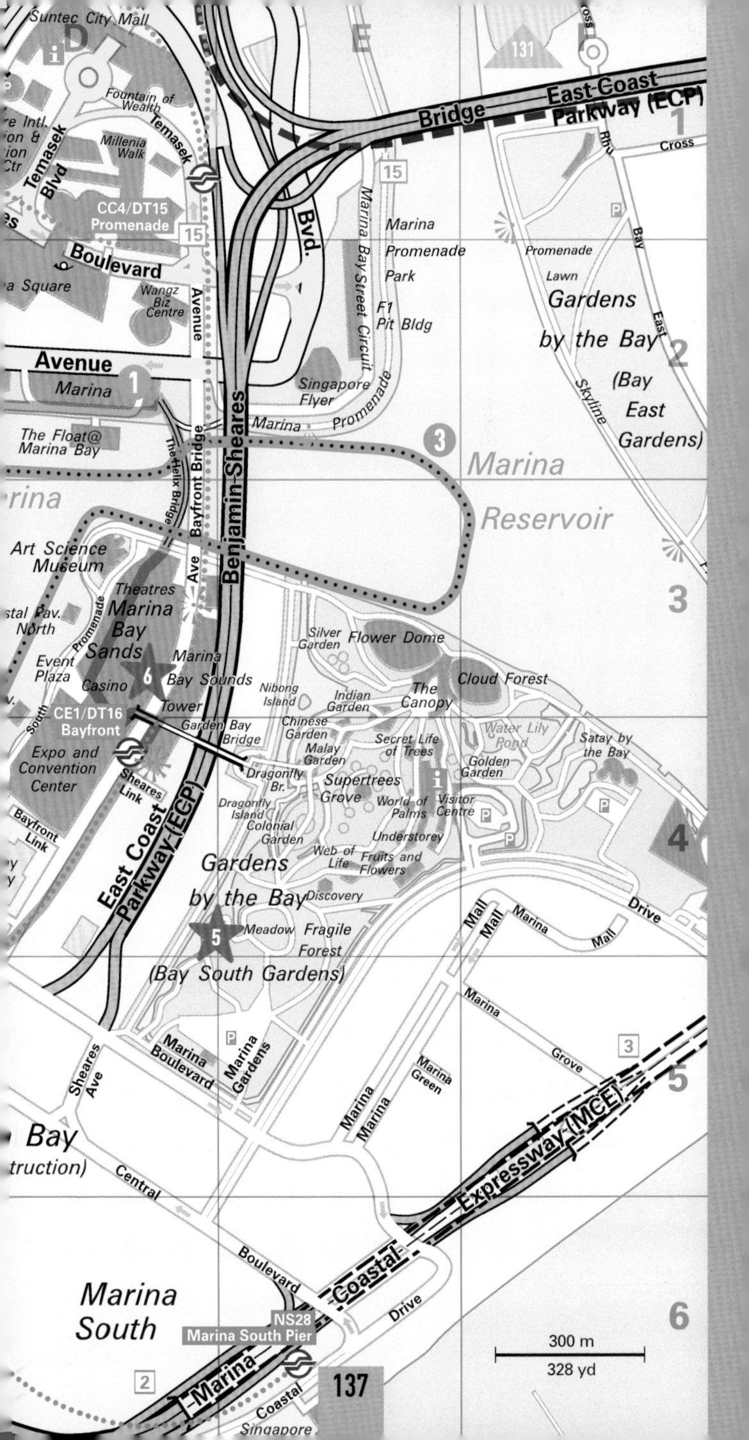

Suntec City Mall
Fountain of Wealth
Temasek
Millenia Walk
Temasek Blvd
CC4/DT15
Promenade
Boulevard
Wangz Biz Centre
Avenue
Marina
The Float@ Marina Bay
The Helix Bridge
Bayfront Bridge
Benjamin Sheares
Bridge
East Coast Parkway (ECP)
Bvd.
Marina Bay Street Circuit
Marina Promenade Park
F1 Pit Bldg
Singapore Flyer
Marina Promenade
Promenade Lawn
Gardens by the Bay (Bay East Gardens)
Skyline
Bay East
Cross
Marina Reservoir
Art Science Museum
Theatres
Marina Bay Sands
Casino
Tower
Event Plaza
Promenade
Marina Bay Sounds
CE1/DT16
Bayfront
Expo and Convention Center
Sheares Link
Bayfront Link
Garden Bay Bridge
Silver Garden
Flower Dome
Cloud Forest
Nibong Island
Indian Garden
The Canopy
Chinese Garden
Malay Garden
Secret Life of Trees
Water Lily Pond
Satay by the Bay
Golden Garden
Dragonfly Br.
Supertrees Grove
World of Palms
Visitor Centre
Dragonfly Island
Colonial Garden
Understorey
Web of Life
Fruits and Flowers
Gardens by the Bay
Discovery
Meadow
Fragile Forest
(Bay South Gardens)
East Coast Parkway (ECP)
Marina Mall
Marina Drive
Marina Grove
Marina Boulevard
Marina Gardens
Sheares Ave
Marina Green
Marina
Bay
Central Boulevard
Expressway (MCE)
Coastal Drive
Marina South
NS28
Marina South Pier
Marina Coastal
300 m
328 yd
131
137

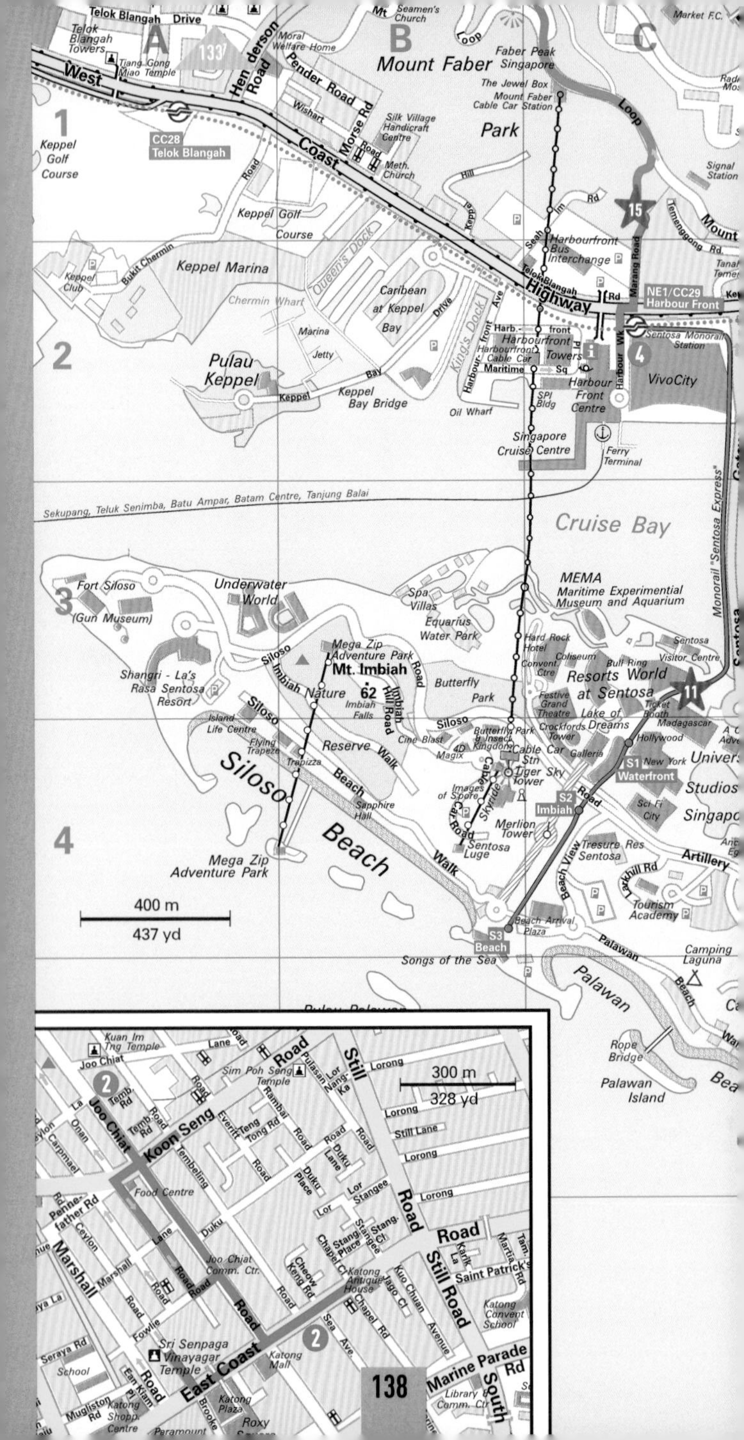

Telok Blangah Drive
Telok Blangah Towers
Tiang Gong Miao Temple
West Coast Highway
Henderson Road
Pender Road
Morse Rd
Moral Welfare Home
Seamen's Church
Mount Faber
Faber Peak Singapore
The Jewel Box
Mount Faber Cable Car Station
Park
Silk Village Handicraft Centre
Meth. Church
CC28 Telok Blangah
Keppel Golf Course
Keppel Marina
Keppel Club
Chermin Wharf
Queen's Dock
Caribean at Keppel Bay
King's Dock
Marina Jetty
Pulau Keppel
Keppel Bay Bridge
Oil Wharf
Harbourfront Bus Interchange
Harbourfront Towers
Harbourfront Cable Car
Maritime Sq
SPI Bldg
Harbour Front Centre
Singapore Cruise Centre
Ferry Terminal
NE1/CC29 Harbour Front
Sentosa Monorail Station
VivoCity
Marang Road
Signal Station
Sekupang, Teluk Senimba, Batu Ampar, Batam Centre, Tanjung Balai
Cruise Bay
Monorail "Sentosa Express"
Fort Siloso (Gun Museum)
Underwater World
Spa Villas
Equarius Water Park
MEMA Maritime Experimental Museum and Aquarium
Mega Zip Adventure Park
Mt. Imbiah
62
Imbiah Falls
Imbiah Hill Road
Imbiah Nature
Shangri - La's Rasa Sentosa Resort
Siloso Road
Island Life Centre
Flying Trapeze
Trapizza
Reserve Walk
Siloso Beach
Sapphire Hall
Butterfly Park
Hard Rock Hotel
Convent Ctre
Coliseum
Bull Ring
Sentosa Visitor Centre
Resorts World at Sentosa
Festive Grand Theatre
Lake of Dreams
Ticket Booth
Madagascar
Crockfords Tower
Galleria
Hollywood
New York
Universal Studios Singapore
S1 Waterfront
S2 Imbiah
Butterfly Park & Insect Kingdom
Cine Blast
4D Magix
Cable Car Stn
Tiger Sky Tower
Images of S'pore
Cable Car Road
Skyride
Merlion Tower
Sentosa Luge
Sci Fi City
Tresure Res Sentosa
Artillery
Larkhill Rd
Beach View
Tourism Academy
Mega Zip Adventure Park
400 m
437 yd
Beach Arrival Plaza
S3 Beach
Songs of the Sea
Palawan Beach
Camping Laguna
Rope Bridge
Palawan Island
Pulau Palawan
Kuan Im Tng Temple
Joo Chiat
Sim Poh Seng Temple
Pulasan
Lor Nang-Ka
Still Road
300 m
328 yd
Lorong
Still Lane
Koon Seng
Teng Tong Rd
Everitt
Rambai
Tembeling
Duku Lane
Duku Place
Lor Stangee
Stang. Place
Stang. Cl
Food Centre
Pennefather Rd
Ceylon
Carpmael
Onan
Marshall
Joo Chiat Comm. Ctr.
Cheow Keng Rd
Chapel Cl
Katong Antique House
Jago Cl
Kuo Chuan Avenue
Saint Patrick's
Martia Rd
Katong Convent School
Fowlie
Sri Senpaga Vinayagar Temple
East Coast Road
Katong Mall
Sea Ave.
Chapel Rd
Seraya Rd
School
Ean Kiam Pl
Mugliston Rd
Katong Shopp. Centre
Katong Plaza
Brooke
Roxy
Paramount
Marine Parade Rd
Library & Comm. Ctr
South

D
E
F
1
2
3
4
5
6
School
Tanah
Kubor Raja
Bukit
Kasita
Rd
Bahru
Kampong
KEPPEL VIADUCT
Keppel
Distripark
Ayer Rajah Expressway
(AYE)
135
2 A
Suzue-PSA
Cold Store
MB 2
Keppel
Workshop
Tanjong Pagar
Distripark
Tanjong Pagar
Complex
Low Hill Rd
Road
Ave
Keppel
Terminal
Avenue
West Coast Highway
Keppel
Wharfes
Bldg
Street 7
Street 6
Tanjong Pagar
Container
Terminal
Road
M
East Wharf
West Wharf
Avenue
N
Gate 2
Brani Terminal
Prima Tower
Terminal
House
West Wharf
Road
Street
J
Keppel
Channel
Brani Terminal Road
Q
Brani
Terminal
Street 9
Brani Terminal Road
Terminal Rd P
Street 8
Pulau Brani
Street 10
R
Terminal
Avenue
Brani Terminal
Building
Avenue
Brani Terminal
Road S
Selat Sengkir
Serapong
Jetty
Maritime
Museum
Sentosa Golf Club
Serapong Course
Ranger Post
Avenue
Road
Historic &
Massacre Site
of Sentosa
Serapong
Lake
Sentosa
Serapong Hill
85
Mt. Serapong
Course
Serapong
Golf
Course
Lakeshore
View
Road
Recycling
Building
SDC
Resorts World
SDC
Transp.Office
Avenue
Spa
Botanica
SDC
Office
Allanbrooke
SDC
Workshop
Serapong
Satellite
Tower
Woodwich
Road
Sentosa
Earth Satellite
Station
Sentosa
Cove Ave
Ocean
Drive
Ocean
Way
Dolphin
Fountain
Sentosa Cove
Arrival Plaza
Coralarium &
Nature Ramble
Road
Allanbrooke
Road
Bukit
The Beaufort
Singapore
The Sentosa
Resort & Spa
Mansi
Tanjong
Beach
Road
Sentosa Golf Club
Tanjong Course
Drive
Sentosa Cove
Sentosa
Golf Club
Walk
Tanjong Beach
Cove Drive
Cove
Ocean Way
Sandy
Bridge
Island
Sandy
Pearl
Bridge
Pearl
Drive
Ocean
Pearl Island
Island
Sandy Island
Way
Cove
Cove
Grove

This index lists a selection of the streets and squares shown in the street atlas

M

N

O

P

Q

R

English / Deutsch	Symbol	Français / Nederlands
Motorway Autobahn		Autoroute Autosnelweg
Road with four lanes Vierspurige Straße		Route à quatre voies Weg met vier rijstroken
Federal road or trunk road Bundes- oder Fernstraße		Route nationale ou à grande circulation Rijksweg of weg voor interlokaal verkeer
Main Road Hauptstraße		Route principale Hoofdweg
Other Roads Sonstige Straßen		Autres routes Overige wegen
Information Information	i	Information Informatie
One way road Einbahnstraße		Rue à sens unique Straat met éénrichtingsverkeer
Pedestrian zone Fußgängerzone		Zone piétonne Voetgangerszone
Main railway with station Hauptbahn mit Bahnhof		Chemin de fer principal avec gare Belangrijke spoorweg met station
Other railways Sonstige Bahnen		Autres lignes Overige spoorwegen
Aerial cableway Kabinenschwebebahn		Téléférique Kabelbaan met cabine
Underground U-Bahn		Métro Ondergrondse spoorweg
Ferry line - Landing stage Fährlinie - Anlegestelle		Ligne de bac - Embarcadère Veerdienst - Aanlegplaats
Church - Church of interest Kirche - Sehenswerte Kirche		Église - Église remarquable Kerk - Bezienswaardige kerk
Synagogue - Mosque Synagoge - Moschee		Synagogue - Mosquée Synagoge - Moskee
Temple - Temple of interest Tempel - Sehenswerter Tempel		Temple - Temple remarquable Tempel - Bezienswaardige tempel
Police station - Post office Polizeistation - Postamt		Poste de police - Bureau de poste Politiebureau - Postkantoor
Parking - Monument Parkplatz - Denkmal	P	Parking - Monument Parkeerplaats - Monument
Hospital Krankenhaus		Hôpital Ziekenhuis
Youth hostel - Camping site Jugendherberge - Campingplatz		Auberge de jeunesse - Terrain de camping Jeugdherberg - Kampeerterrein
Built-up area - Public building Bebaute Fläche - Öffentliches Gebäude		Zone bâtie - Bâtiment public Bebouwing - Openbaar gebouw
Industrial area Industriegelände		Zone industrielle Industrieterrein
Park, forest Park, Wald		Parc, bois Park, bos
Beach Strand		Plage Strand
Restricted traffic zone Zone mit Verkehrsbeschränkungen		Circulation réglementée par de péages Zone met Verkeersbeperkingen
MARCO POLO Discovery Tour 1 MARCO POLO Erlebnistour 1		MARCO POLO Tour d'aventure 1 MARCO POLO Avontuurlijke Route 1
MARCO POLO Discovery Tours MARCO POLO Erlebnistouren		MARCO POLO Tours d'aventure MARCO POLO Avontuurlijke Routes
MARCO POLO Highlight	1	MARCO POLO Highlight

INDEX

This index lists all sights, destinations and beaches, plus the names of important streets, places, names and key words featured in this guide.
Numbers in bold indicate a main entry

WRITE TO US

e-mail: info@marcopologuides.co.uk

Did you have a great holiday?
Is there something on your mind?
Whatever it is, let us know!
Whether you want to praise, alert us to errors or give us a personal tip – MARCO POLO would be pleased to hear from you.
We do everything we can to provide the very latest information for your trip. Nevertheless, despite all of our authors' thorough research, errors can creep in. MARCO POLO does not accept any liability for this. Please contact us by e-mail or post.

MARCO POLO Travel Publishing Ltd
Pinewood, Chineham Business Park
Crockford Lane, Chineham
Basingstoke, Hampshire RG24 8AL
United Kingdom

PICTURE CREDITS
Cover photograph: Marina Bay Sands Hotel (Look: Stumpe)
Photos: Corbis/Reuters: E. Su (68); R. Freyer (7, 11, 25, 26/27, 33, 48/49, 59, 60, 70 left, 72/73, 84, 90/91, 97, 98/99); Getty Images: R. M. Gill (9, 30, 114/115); huber-images: M. Borchi (47), M. Rellini (4 bottom, 5, 12/13, 42), Scatà (92), Schmid (front flap, left, front flap, right, 4 top, 10, 20/21, 37, 40, 51, 54, 56/57, 70 right, 118 top), R. Schmid (2/3, 14/15, 62/63, 82/83); M. Kirchgessner (114); Look: Stumpe (1 top); mauritius images/Alamy (6, 8, 18 top, 18 bottom, 22, 35, 38, 44, 52, 64, 67, 76, 79, 80, 87, 95, 104, 110, 113, 118 bottom, 119, 130/131); mauritius images/ib: Stengert (17); mauritius images/Imagebroker/gourmet-vision (19 top); mauritius images/Prisma (74); mauritius images/Westend 61 (19 bottom); mauritius images/Ypps (18 centre); A. M. Mosler (89, 115); White Star: Reichelt (116, 116/117, 117)

2nd Edition 2017
fully revised and updated
Worldwide Distribution: Marco Polo Travel Publishing Ltd, Pinewood, Chineham Business Park, Crockford Lane, Basingstoke, Hampshire RG24 8AL, United Kingdom. Email: sales@marcopolouk.com

Chief editors: Marion Zorn (concept, text editor)
Authors: Rainer Wolfgramm, Sabine and Dr. Christoph Hein; editor: Christina Sothmann
Programme supervision: Susanne Heimburger, Tamara Hub, Nikolai Michaelis, Kristin Schimpf, Martin Silbermann
Picture editor: Gabriele Forst
What's hot: wunder media, Munich
Cartography street atlas & pull-out map: © MAIRDUMONT, Ostfildern
Design: milchhof : atelier, Berlin; Front cover, pull-out map cover, page 1: factor product munich
Discovery Tours: Susan Chaaban, Dipl.-Des. (FH)
Translated from German by Robert Scott McInnes, Jane Riester; editor of the English edition: Sarah Trenker, Marlis von Hessert-Fraatz
Prepress: Bintang Buchservice GmbH, Berlin

Printed in China

DOS & DON'TS

A few things you should bear in mind in Singapore

DON'T BRING DRUGS

Do not even think about it: there are draconian punishments for even the smallest amount of drugs (e.g. designer drugs, hashish, cocaine, heroin) in Singapore, including the death penalty – and they also apply to foreigners. Merely being in possession is enough to get you into trouble.

DON'T GO ON AN EXCURSION AT THE WEEKEND

From Saturday at noon to Sunday evening, hundreds of thousands of Singaporeans flock to all of the excursion destinations you also want to visit. If at all possible, try to visit them during the week from Monday to Friday.

DON'T SMOKE OR EAT CHEWING GUM

Smoking in air-conditioned restaurants, public buildings and lifts is forbidden – and the fine can amount to 1000 S$. The famous ban on chewing gum was eased after twelve years: you can now buy two kinds of chewing gum 'for medicinal purposes' in chemist's shops – for example, as a substitute for nicotine for those trying to give up smoking. But, you are naturally still not allowed to spit it out on the street.

DON'T GET TAKEN IN BY RIP-OFF ARTISTS AND TOUTS

Be careful of 'special' offers that initially appear to be extremely reasonable. They often turn out to be a rip-off. This can apply to tailors or the 'English student's' free tour of the city. It is the same with the touts who talk to you on the street 'Copy watch? T-shirts? Girls?' The *Official Singapore Guide,* which you can get free of charge at the airport, lists all those shops with the so-called *Singapore Gold Circle* guaranteeing their trustworthiness and quality.

DON'T UNDERESTIMATE THE SUN AND HEAT

Singapore is on the equator. The sun is scorching even when the sky is cloudy. You should also not forget that you will sweat a great deal – in spite of the high humidity. Drink a lot and often – at least three litres is recommended. Use suncreams with a high protection factor. You can buy them in all chemist's shops in Singapore – and usually cheaper than at home.

DON'T TOUCH!

Some women try to blackmail foreign men by claiming that they have been sexually harrassed. You could be faced with legal proceedings and high fines. Just brushing against someone in the underground or disco can be enough. Keep your distance!